IMMERSION
Bible Studies

PROVERBS, ECCLESIASTES, SONG OF SOLOMON

Frank Ramirez

Abingdon Press

Nashville

PROVERBS, ECCLESIASTES, SONG OF SOLOMON
IMMERSION BIBLE STUDIES
by Frank Ramirez

Copyright © 2011 by Abingdon Press

Library of Congress Cataloging-in-Publication Data

Ramirez, Frank, 1954-
  Proverbs, Ecclesiastes, Song of Solomon / Frank Ramirez.
    p. cm. — (Immersion Bible studies)
  ISBN 978-1-4267-1631-7 (curriculum—printed/text plus : alk. paper) 1. Bible. O.T. Proverbs—Textbooks. 2. Bible. O.T. Proverbs—Criticism, interpretation, etc. 3. Bible. O.T. Ecclesiastes—Textbooks. 4. Bible. O.T. Ecclesiastes—Criticism, interpretation, etc. 5. Bible. O.T. Song of Solomon—Textbooks. 6. Bible. O.T. Song of Solomon—Criticism, interpretation, etc. I. Title.
  BS1465.67.R36 2011
  223'.06—dc23

                                                              2011022893

Editor: Stan Purdum
Leader Guide Writer: Martha Bettis Gee

11 12 13 14 15 16 17 18 19 20—10 9 8 7 6 5 4 3 2 1

Contents

REVIEW TEAM

Diane Blum
Pastor
East End United Methodist Church
Nashville, Tennessee

Susan Cox
Pastor
McMurry United Methodist Church
Claycomo, Missouri

Margaret Ann Crain
Professor of Christian Education
Garrett-Evangelical Theological Seminary
Evanston, Illinois

Nan Duerling
Curriculum Writer and Editor
Cambridge, Maryland

Paul Escamilla
Pastor and Writer
St. John's United Methodist Church
Austin, Texas

James Hawkins
Pastor and Writer
Smyrna, Delaware

Andrew Johnson
Professor of New Testament
Nazarene Theological Seminary
Kansas City, Missouri

Snehlata Patel
Pastor
Woodrow United Methodist Church
Staten Island, New York

Emerson B. Powery
Professor of New Testament
Messiah College
Grantham, Pennsylvania

Clayton Smith
Pastoral Staff
Church of the Resurrection
Leawood, Kansas

Harold Washington
Professor of Hebrew Bible
Saint Paul School of Theology
Kansas City, Missouri

Carol Wehrheim
Curriculum Writer and Editor
Princeton, New Jersey

IMMERSION
Bible Studies

PROVERBS, ECCLESIASTES, SONG OF SOLOMON

Praise for IMMERSION

"IMMERSION BIBLE STUDIES is a powerful tool in helping readers to hear God speak through Scripture and to experience a deeper faith as a result."
Adam Hamilton, author of *24 Hours That Changed the World*

"This unique Bible study makes Scripture come alive for students. Through the study, students are invited to move beyond the head into the heart of faith."
Bishop Joseph W. Walker, author of *Love and Intimacy*

"If you're looking for a deeper knowledge and understanding of God's Word, you must dive into IMMERSION BIBLE STUDIES. Whether in a group setting or as an individual, you will experience God and his unconditional love for each of us in a whole new way."
Pete Wilson, founding and senior pastor of Cross Point Church

"This beautiful series helps readers become fluent in the words and thoughts of God, for purposes of illumination, strength building, and developing a closer walk with the One who loves us so."
Laurie Beth Jones, author of *Jesus, CEO* and *The Path*

"The IMMERSION BIBLE STUDIES series is no less than a game changer. It ignites the purpose and power of Scripture by showing us how to do more than just know God or love God; it gives us the tools to love like God as well."
Shane Stanford, author of *You Can't Do Everything . . . So Do Something*

Immersion Bible Studies

*A fresh new look at the Bible, from beginning to end,
and what it means in your life.*

Welcome to Immersion!

We've asked some of the leading Bible scholars, teachers, and pastors to help us with a new kind of Bible study. Immersion remains true to Scripture but always asks, "Where are you in your life? What do you struggle with? What makes you rejoice?" Then it helps you read the Scriptures to discover their deep, abiding truths. Immersion is about God and God's Word, and it is also about you—not just your thoughts, but your feelings and your faith.

In each study you will prayerfully read the Scripture and reflect on it. Then you will engage it in three ways:

Claim Your Story
> Through stories and questions, think about your life, with its struggles and joys.

Enter the Bible Story
> Explore Scripture and consider what God is saying to you.

Live the Story
> Reflect on what you have discovered, and put it into practice in your life.

IMMERSION makes use of an exciting new translation of Scripture, the Common English Bible (CEB). The CEB and IMMERSION BIBLE STUDIES will offer adults:

- the emotional expectation to find the love of God
- the rational expectation to find the knowledge of God
- reliable, genuine, and credible power to transform lives
- clarity of language

Whether you are using the Common English Bible or another translation, IMMERSION BIBLE STUDIES will offer a refreshing plunge into God's Word, your life, and your life with God.

1.

Read the Handbook

Proverbs 1–9

Claim Your Story

My grandmother Maria Galvan Ramirez was born in Mexico in 1900 but crossed the border north to the United States when she was ten. Her father, a military officer, refused to kill civilians during the Mexican Revolution.

She brought folk wisdom with her. What I remember best was a little poem she'd recite when we'd run indoors following a fall. Grandma Mary would wave her hand over the wound and recite,

> *Sana, sana,*
> *Colita de rana.*
> *Si no sanas hoy*
> *Sanarás mañana.*

A *sana, sana* was usually enough medicine to make everything all better. The first two lines were silly: "Wellness, wellness, gas from a frog." But the kernel of truth was in the last two lines: "If you don't get well today, you'll get well tomorrow."

Not always, of course. A *sana, sana* won't fix broken bones; but for most things it worked pretty well. That's what wisdom is all about. It's sensible. It works most of the time.

It's the same with biblical wisdom, which fits most, but not all, situations, as we'll discover as we study Proverbs.

What wisdom did you learn from your parents, grandparents, or guardians that worked most of the time? Was there a time it didn't help? If so, why?

Enter the Bible Story

The first time I drove across the Bonneville Salt Flats west of Salt Lake City, I was astounded by how flat and featureless a trackless waste could be—a perfect and absolute blank, without landmarks. It passed in a haze.

But as family business caused me to drive across it once a year for a decade and a half, my perception changed. I gradually recognized landmarks and could accurately gauge where I was without cheating and looking at the mile markers. The Salt Flats became a place.

The first time I read through the Bible from start to finish, as a teenager in high school, I have to admit that the Book of Proverbs also passed in kind of a haze. In its own way, it too was a trackless waste. There was one proverb after another, all sounding kind of the same. Nag, nag, nag. When I finished the book, I wondered what I had read and could not have told you where to find any particular proverb.

Yet over the years as I came to understand the structure of the book, it all started to make sense. As a result, I now enjoy Proverbs—not just the book, but the proverbs themselves.

Why proverbs? Why do we need them? What good do they do? Let me make a couple of suggestions.

First, we're not all born knowing this stuff. Someone has to tell us common sense before it's common enough for us to be sensible.

Second, I'm reminded of what the Quakers say when someone tries to play situation ethics with them: "I may not know what I will do in a particular situation, but I know which way I want to lean." Learning a proverb may help us make wise choices at crunch time. That's why George Washington as a young man carefully copied into a little book rules to live by. Always conscious of his lack of formal education, he strongly believed that proper conduct and decorum could be learned and if learned, would stand him in good stead for all his life.

Washington's rules for living came from three sources: Seneca's *Morals*, a book called *The Rules of Civility*, and the play *Cato* by Joseph Addison. Washington memorized sentences such as the lofty thoughts "An honest man can never be outdone in courtesy" and "The contempt of death makes all the miseries of life easy to us," as well as more practical matters like "Rinse not your mouth in the Presence of Others" and "Spit not in the Fire." These proverbs guided his conduct his entire life and caused others to think highly of him in all circumstances.

What were the sources of common sense in your life? Your family? a mentor? a book? How seriously did you take them at first?

Cut to Fit

Like Washington's little book, biblical proverbs are drawn from several sources and deal with the lofty and the commonplace. The biblical proverbs were preserved because they are valuable. If we learn them, they'll be there when we need them.

God teaches through both revealed and natural religion. Revealed religion is, as the name suggests, a revelation from outside the natural universe. Natural religion is what we can deduce about God and godly living from the world around us. Though we're used to thinking of divine revelation coming with dramatic bells and whistles, good, old-fashioned, hardheaded common sense doesn't require fireworks, just our intention to study and learn. Indeed, "wisdom" could be another name for natural religion.

The Book of Proverbs is part of the Wisdom tradition in the Bible. The thing about wisdom is that it requires a hands-on approach. It's up to us to evaluate whether a kernel of wisdom applies to the situation in which we find ourselves. Not all wisdom applies to all situations.

For instance, the two back-to-back sayings in Proverbs 26:4-5 sound contradictory. What this tells us, however, is that when it comes to wisdom, one size doesn't fit all. In the first proverb, we are told, "Don't answer fools according to their folly" and in the second, "Answer fools according to their folly." In each case, a reason is given why one should choose to act or not act that way. In the first case, we don't answer fools because we'll end up acting like them. In the second instance, we *do* answer or else they'll interpret our silence to mean they're wise. It's up to us to evaluate the situation and choose which one applies to the moment.

"The Lord helps those who help themselves" is a fine proverb (not a biblical proverb) to encourage us to be self-starters, but those whose disabilities require at least some assistance to maintain independence might find it has a hollow ring. And I wonder what the creator of that proverb would have thought of the saying "Don't click send" (a more modern version of "Look before you leap"), which is more appropriate to our era of e-mail, Twitter, and Facebook.

Think of a saying that you learned as a child. Has it stood the test of time? In what circumstance does it apply?

The First Edition

The Hebrew word translated as "proverbs" refers to more than just pithy sayings. It can refer to stories, sayings, warnings, and even poems and songs (like a *sana, sana*). These maxims are part of the wealth of wisdom all cultures accumulate. But why was this set of proverbs gathered together in the biblical Book of Proverbs?

Most experts agree that Proverbs was originally compiled as an "Instruction Manual for Civil Servants" in the court of King Solomon. Young men (and they all were men) who sought to advance in the life of the royal court needed to know how to behave.

Although the book is attributed to Solomon, who was famed for his wisdom, it seems plausible, considering differences in language, tone, and intent, that this collection of inspired literature also includes a good deal of wisdom from many centuries, including that of King Hezekiah, one of the few reformers during the time of the kings. And it is also quite possible that the book was not put together in its present form until after the people of God returned from exile in Babylon.

In some cases, such as the Thirty Sayings (Proverbs 22:17–24:22), discussed in Chapter 4 of this study, the source for some proverbs is precisely known. The source for others may be guessed at. Regardless, their incorporation into the Bible gives them special significance for us.

By Any Other Name

There are only three places in Proverbs where God is referred to as *Elohim*, the Hebrew word for the concept of God. Everywhere else God is *Yahweh* (built around the verb for "I Am" and translated as "LORD"), the personal name of a personal God. This is appropriate for a book that is practical and personal.

The blurb of a book is often its strongest selling point. In a few words, the potential reader discovers what the book is all about. The first seven verses of Proverbs are like a blurb. They tell us that the purpose of the book "is to teach wisdom and discipline" as well as to "understand wise sayings" (1:2). This instruction, which "is righteous, just, and full of integrity," will "make the naïve mature, / the young knowledgeable and discreet" (1:3-4).

The key ingredient in this book is our reverence for God as the source of this wisdom. "Wisdom begins with the fear of the LORD, / but fools despise wisdom and instruction" (Proverbs 1:7), states our blurb. This is the first step to a disciplined, well-lived life. Honoring and respecting the Creator is essential in appreciating wisdom because, given the choice, wouldn't we rather be wise than foolish?

As stated earlier, we find God through revelation; but the authors of these proverbs knew that we find God in the natural universe as well. Proverbs tells us that "it's useless to cast a net in the sight of a bird" (1:17). This observation warns us that we'd better assume that those who set a trap for us aren't going to act in plain sight either, as the next two verses declare (1:18-19). There are people who actually are out to get us, wisdom warns. Don't assume everyone is as nice as we are.

Actual scientific accuracy isn't always the point in natural observations. "Go to the ant, you lazy person," we are told; "observe its ways and grow wise" (Proverbs 6:6). This is a good example of how a writer might include scientifically inaccurate information but still have something important to say. The proverb continues,

> The ant has no commander, officer, or ruler.
> Even so, it gets its food in summer;
> gathers its provisions at harvest. (6:7-8)

That's not strictly true. There's a queen to each colony, and the complex scents used by ants direct their activities in a logical manner. Regardless of all that, the point being made is still valid.

I Hear You Calling

We find more than just proverbs in the first nine chapters of this biblical book. There are songs in praise of wisdom, both in the form of teachings we can learn and personified as a living presence that loves us and pleads with us to listen.

In his song "Where Have All the Flowers Gone?" folk singer Pete Seeger asks continually, "When will they ever learn?" This is the same question asked about us by the character named Wisdom, who is represented as a woman in these first nine chapters.

We first meet Wisdom in Proverbs 1:20-21, where she calls out at "the entrances of the city gates" for our attention. In biblical times, the gates of a city were where old men met to share their wisdom and to settle disputes, the same way older folks gather at a coffee shop nowadays to solve the world's problems. It is interesting to find a woman in a man's preserve.

The city gates are a symbol of the ordinary places where we spend our time. The struggle between good and evil takes place in the real world, not in some vague spiritual realm. Wisdom's realm is a world of free will and choice.

To the Hebrew way of thinking, there are real choices to be made. Wisdom speaks of two paths: a way of good and a way of evil. This sort of choice requires free will. The arena for our free will is the universe as God created it. This universe plays fair with us; if we learn the rules, we'll do OK.

In our first meeting with Wisdom, she taunts, though she seems to expect she will be ignored. When we meet her again in Proverbs 8, she is pleading out of love and concern. Then, in her cosmic autobiography, we

Replace All

I'm not sure if there are many hymns written about wisdom. However, I got to thinking about the lyrics to the hymn "Softly and Tenderly Jesus Is Calling," written by Will L. Thompson. You know, if you substituted, just one time, the word *wisdom* for Jesus, you'd get a hymn that sounds a lot like Proverbs 8. No. Really.

learn that Wisdom has been around since Creation. Why is this so important? This is important because in the competing mythologies of the ancient world, Creation was inexplicable, sometimes an accident. The gods might be immortal, but they could not fully control the larger cosmos. Chaos could always intrude. The universe might dissolve.

God created the world with wisdom; so we are assured that the building project to beat all building projects is secure, well planned, well wrought, perfectly established.

> I was there when he established the heavens,
>   when he marked out the horizon on the deep sea,
> when he thickened the clouds above,
>   when he secured the fountains of the deep,
> when he set a limit for the sea....
>   I was beside him as a master of crafts.
>   (Proverbs 8:27-30)

The perspective of Wisdom Literature is that the wisdom that undergirds the universe ensures that not fate or chance, but our choices for good or ill will be the determining factor in our lives.

Certainly, that's the intent of proverbs that warn the budding civil servants against being led astray by sexual temptations (see Proverbs 2:16; 5:3-4, 20; 9:13-18, among others). The image of the foreign woman points not only literally to someone who might seduce them, but sometimes to a woman named Folly (9:13). Figuratively, she represents the impact of other cultures that might tempt them from the fear of the Lord. Yet wisdom in the form of proverbs borrowed from those other cultures also appears in this book. This is an example of the way readers must grapple with the proverbs that are presented and determine if they suit their circumstances.

This lesson is extremely important when it comes to the uncomfortable use of the images of women as wicked temptresses—although it must be remembered that this is balanced by the image of a feminine personification of Wisdom, as well as by the competent household manager portrayed in Proverbs 31:10-31. Remember that Proverbs was originally written for young men. Perhaps if these proverbs had been written for young women, there would also be warnings about sly men waiting to lead them astray.

Read through the first nine chapters of Proverbs. Mark down those proverbs that seem to apply to you. Note also those that do not seem useful. When might they prove useful to you? Are there images with which you are not comfortable? If so, how would you change those images so you would get the same lesson?

The Search Engine in Your Head

I like the way so many of the proverbs speak directly to the way we ought to live. "Don't withhold good from someone who deserves it, / when it is in your power to do so" (Proverbs 3:27) is immediately followed by an admonition that could have come straight out of the Gospels:

> Don't say to your neighbor,
> "Go and come back; I'll give it to you tomorrow,"
> when you have it. (3:28)

We also meet in this first section a type of proverb that was very common, sometimes called the "counting proverb." The sage tells us we will be given a number of examples that prove a point, and in the following line that number is raised by one to emphasize the point. So we read, "There are six things that the LORD hates, / seven things detestable to him" (Proverbs 6:16).

Across the Testaments

Measure Twice, Cut Once

The LORD laid the foundations of the earth with wisdom,
establishing the heavens with understanding.
(Proverbs 3:19)

Wisdom's place in the created order is reminiscent of the way Jesus is described as the Word in the Gospel of John:

The Word was with God in the beginning.
Everything came into being through the Word
and without the Word nothing came into being.
(John 1:2-3)

"Get wisdom; get understanding" (Proverbs 4:5), we are told. In other words, wisdom can be taught. We may not know this stuff yet, but there's hope for us because we can learn. This implies that our character is not frozen. Our lives can be transformed. That's the important thing to remember about wisdom. It can be learned.

I'm reminded of Abraham Lincoln's determination to learn, despite his lack of opportunity. Because of his lack of formal education, he tirelessly studied the Bible and Shakespeare so that he could quote from them with ease when he needed them. His great speeches relied on those cadences. His desire to acquire wisdom meant Lincoln usually had the right phrase mentally at hand.

We can grow and we can learn if we reverence God as the source of wisdom. There's hope in this, hope for us.

Describe the ways God's Word was presented to you and how you were told it was to be used. How is this different from the idea of biblical wisdom and the manner in which it is to be interpreted?

Live the Story

My grandmother didn't corner the market on wisdom, of course. My late mother-in-law, who was born in Nebraska, had a lot of good sayings too, including one she used when people got their noses bent out of joint: "They've got the same clothes to get glad in they got mad in."

Yet, as is often the case with wisdom, just because you know something doesn't mean you live it. I remember the eight years when my mother-in-law didn't speak to two of her brothers even though everyone lived within a few miles of each other. It was no good quoting her own saying back to her, either. We had to wait for her to be ready to hear it. Thank heaven those bridges were finally mended!

That's the thing about wisdom. For it to work, we not only have to listen but also to hear. We've got to chew up and digest wisdom for it to work in our lives.

Can you think of a time when wisdom—or common sense—told you that you were in the wrong, but you hated to admit it? Why is it hard to apply proverbs to ourselves? How necessary is a good sense of humor for us to admit our own faults?

2.

This or That

Proverbs 10–15

Claim Your Story

I learned how to drive in Los Angeles, long before GPS. I learned to navigate by keeping the mountains in sight. It was even easier when I lived in Indiana. The roads in Elkhart County were laid out in a grid of one-mile squares. Wrong turn? No problem. A few turns and you're back on the right track.

Now I live in the Appalachian Mountains of middle Pennsylvania. If you get on the wrong road, you are on the wrong road. The farther you go, the more you're lost. You can't work your way back to the right road by going forward. You have to turn around and go back the way you came.

Sometimes wisdom is easy to navigate. Keep in mind some basic landmarks ("The beginning of wisdom is the fear of the LORD" [Proverbs 9:10].) and you'll be back on track in no time. In some cases, however, if you've strayed, it's going to take some doing, going laboriously all the way back the way you came.

Think of some different course corrections you have made in your life. What wisdom guided you? How easy was it to change the direction you were going? Did you ever get really lost? Was someone there to guide you or at least point out the landmarks?

Enter the Bible Story

So here we are. At last. The real deal. The proverbs of Solomon, that great and glorious king, the one who built the Temple, the one who said,

"Give me a sword, and we'll give half a baby to each of the plaintiffs" (paraphrase of 1 Kings 3:24-25).

Solomon's wisdom was legendary. And there is every reason to believe that many of the proverbs in this section of the book were either written by Solomon, repeated by Solomon, or prized by Solomon and his court.

These proverbs are exquisitely timeless, so it would be very difficult to prove in what era they originated. In fact, it's really not that important when they were written or by whom. Wisdom is about utility, not about authorship.

Those who compiled this collection of proverbs, both during the reign of Solomon and later, during the reign of the reformer Hezekiah (see Proverbs 25:1), weren't worried about crediting an author, footnoting each verse, or taking credit for themselves. They wanted to put together the ultimate self-help guide, teaching us how to make choices using our free will so that we might live righteously and well.

Proverbs 10–15, the core of the book, consists almost exclusively of what are known as antithetical sayings. That is to say, each verse (The verse numberings were added centuries later, so don't place too much reliance on them.) is a two-line poem. The first line expresses something either positive or negative, and the second line makes an opposite state-ment that is either negative or positive. For instance:

> Laziness brings poverty;
> hard work makes one rich. (Proverbs 10:4)

Or:

> Those who love discipline love knowledge,
> and those who hate correction are stupid.
> (Proverbs 12:1)

This is classic wisdom, laying out a choice for people to make. Even though we've all known exceptions to these rules, in the long run, they prove true.

I can testify that hard work made me rich—not in cash, but in contentment. The second proverb speaks more clearly to me. As a writer, I have enjoyed being a part of writers groups that provided honest but tough criticism. I've come to discover that everyone needs someone to tell them, when appropriate, that what they're planning to do is not a good idea. Yet many people resist hearing any sort of correction or criticism. They react with hostility. I'm reminded of the Wicked Witch in the musical *The Wiz*, where she sings, "Don't nobody tell me no bad news."

Interpret the two proverbs above based on your personal experience. What sort of work do you do? Is hard work always rewarded? What are your hobbies? How do you receive and give criticism?

What Really Matters

I love peanuts. I love Brazil nuts. You can munch peanuts by the handful. Brazil nuts take time to crack open, and they're rich enough that you eat them one at a time.

Some books can be read swiftly. But the proverbs in the Bible are Brazil nuts. Each one is carefully thought out, tested over centuries, preserved, and protected. You can stand by a proverb. Each one is tried and true.

Proverbs are short, but they are not like Tweets or Twitters—brief, often full of misspellings and abbreviations, transitory, blurted out with-

---

Across the Testaments

Proverbs II: The Sequel

The New Testament book most like Proverbs is the Letter of James. Like Proverbs, it is a wisdom book that presents us with two choices: a way of life and a way of death. For example, Proverbs specifically speaks about the danger of improper speech (see, among many others, Proverbs 10:11, 19, 31, 32; 12:23; 13:5; 15:28). James also warns on several occasions about the damage the tongue can do (see James 1:26; 3:5-6, 8). But he is at his best when he paraphrases Jesus and warns us not to swear at all, but to let our yes be yes and our no be no (see James 5:12; compare Matthew 5:37).

out thinking, then apologized for and withdrawn in embarrassment. Biblical proverbs have weight. They last.

Not all contemporary wisdom stands the test of time. The humorist Hilaire Belloc was famous for two lines that, though he may have meant them satirically, were taken seriously by many in the British Empire as a symbol of their enduring supremacy.

Taken from a larger poem, the couplet went,

> Whatever happens, we have got
> The Maxim gun, and they have not.[1]

The Maxim gun was one of the first reliable machine guns, and it was used to devastating effect in the colonial wars in Africa during the late nineteenth and early twentieth centuries. However, like all weapons, its supremacy was brief; and it was soon replaced by even ghastlier weapons of war. Today that proverb might be considered true because it proves the opposite of its original intent, that in the end nothing can prop up or maintain colonial governments forever.

Jump around these six chapters and mark with a highlighter selected proverbs that intrigue you. Consider these choices and why they caught your eye. How true are the words of these proverbs for you? When do they apply to your life? When are they not of much use? Which are peanuts? Which are Brazil nuts?

Why We're Here

One thing you can't help but notice as you read Proverbs: Some themes occur over and over again. Also, the proverbs don't seem to appear in any particular order. One can imagine that a modern-day editor would insist that the author organize them by categories or, at the very least, include an index so each would be easy to find.

As mentioned before, the Book of Proverbs is believed to be a training manual for young men preparing to serve in the royal court. One recurring theme, consistent with the book's intent to teach us to live well and righteously, is establishing justice for the purpose of maintaining order.

That was an aim of the royal court. That should be one of our aims as individuals and as a church.

Take Proverbs 15:25, for example: "The LORD snatches away the arrogant one's house, / but he preserves the widow's boundaries." No doubt many widows in ancient Israel suffered injustice. That's why Jesus would speak centuries later in a parable about a widow pestering an unjust judge until she got her way (Luke 18:1-8). The rights of the powerless must be upheld by those in authority because that's what God does, and that's what God expects of us.

Contrast this with the saying that some people wryly call the *real* Golden Rule: "Whoever has the gold makes the rules." That sentiment, which is not biblical, may describe the world as observed by some; but it is not the world as we expect and want it to be.

One imagines that after a proverb was read aloud in ancient times, the group would discuss various cases that might have come up and other theoretical situations that could have been imagined. A single two-line poem might well have inspired many minutes, or even hours, of lively debate.

It was necessary during these discussions for all involved to have heart—but not heart as we know it. The Hebrew word for "heart" appears ninety-nine times in Proverbs, but there is a reason it is sometimes translated as "mind" or "sense" in the Common English Bible. The ancients—not just those in the Jewish world—looked on the heart as the seat not only of emotions but also of rational thought and judgment. We tend to split the two. We talk about using our brains versus acting out of our heart. In Proverbs, not just the emotions or feelings but also wisdom and thought had their source in the heart. So Proverbs 7:7 reads,

> I looked among the naïve young men
> and noticed among the youth,
> one who had no *sense*. (italics added)

In Proverbs 4:23 we are told to "protect your *mind*, for life flows from it" (italics added). In Proverbs the heart feeds all facets of life.

The proverbs fit many different categories of wisdom, covering personal behavior, corporate behavior, economics, morality, agriculture, manners, words, and deeds; but underlying all of these is the concept of the fear of the Lord. What does that mean?

In the movie *The Wizard of Oz*, the travelers are initially in great fear of the wizard, who is revealed technologically with explosions, lightning, and other impressive bells and whistles. Once the travelers get past all that, however, the wizard isn't all that impressive.

The people of God in the Bible—like us—sometimes experienced God through fireworks and earthquakes, through miracles and wonders. They also experienced God through his commands and his concern. The difference (not the only difference of course!) between God and the wizard is that even when one gets past all the frightening elements on Mount Sinai, the fear, the respect, for God only grows. The fear of the Lord in Proverbs is associated with knowledge. Truly to know God is to grow in awe. But this awe, this fear if you will, is still associated with love: God's love for us and our love for God.

Have you ever been up in an airplane, feeling just fine, when suddenly you realized there was nothing between you and the earth but a very thin layer of metal and thousands of feet of empty air? The vision can be startling and very uncomfortable, but it can also give you an emotional appreciation of what should never seem ordinary. Instead of complaining about your legroom and the fact you don't get a free bag of peanuts, you suddenly realize what an awe-inspiring situation you're in.

Not all of us experience glory under the same circumstances. The first time I saw the Grand Canyon, I was so overwhelmed by the scale, the distance, the magnificence, I nearly fainted. I couldn't breathe. I couldn't move. No photograph had prepared me for the overwhelming wonder. At the same time, other tourists just stood around getting in each other's way trying to take pictures, totally unimpressed. (My youngest son, for instance, who was only three years old at the time, was so unimpressed that he tried to climb a fence to go down into the canyon. You think I was afraid before…)

When—through a verse of Scripture, the presence of a true if unheralded saint, the glory of creation, an epiphany during worship—have you had a glimpse of God's true glory? When have you been overwhelmed with a loving fear of the Lord? Or have you ever had such an experience? Is it easy, or even possible, to put such an experience into words?

As you read Proverbs, underline or highlight all verses that use the phrase "the fear of the LORD." What do these verses have in common? What are the differences?

Chosen at Random

If I were to try to write a commentary on each poem in Proverbs, this guide would involve more than immersion; it might require life vests. So I have picked out a few that intrigued me. You may have a different response to these proverbs, and that's definitely allowed.

> The LORD detests dishonest scales,
>   but delights in an accurate weight.
>   (Proverbs 11:1)

Dishonest scales were no doubt a fact of ordinary life, but this proverb lifts a petty crime into the realm of divine justice and reminds us that God's anger is directed at those who cheat others.

> When the righteous succeed, a city rejoices;
>   when the wicked perish, there are shouts of joy.
>   (Proverbs 11:10)

Joy and rejoicing result from two very different situations. The ultimate legacy of saints and sinners may have little to do with their current fortunes. Even if evil seems to be succeeding in this life, in the long run history tends to vindicate the just and condemn the unjust. The long view matters.

> Like a gold ring in a pig's nose
>   is a beautiful woman who lacks discretion.
>   (Proverbs 11:22)

But I'll bet the same goes for a handsome guy who also lacks common sense. Women in those days adorned themselves with nose rings. I like the way humor is used in Proverbs. The image of a pig wearing a gold ring brings us up short, and laughter only emphasizes that the proverb says something significant.

> People curse those who hoard grain,
> but bless those who sell it. (Proverbs 11:26)

Putting oneself and personal profit before the good of the group is simply wrong. No one is trying to stop us from making a profit selling grain during tough times, but there is a limit to legitimate gain.

The next two are related.

> The righteous care about their livestock's needs,
> but even the compassion of the wicked is cruel.
> (Proverbs 12:10)

And:

> When there are no oxen, the stall is clean,
> but when there is a strong bull,
> there is abundant produce.
> (Proverbs 14:4)

The way we treat animals says a lot about the way we treat people. In the case of the second proverb above, if we take on the responsibility of animal ownership, then we need to take care of the animal. There's an old Native American proverb that when we die, we will be met at the bridge leading to the eternal hunting grounds by all the animals whose lives we've intersected; and it's up to them to decide if we cross over.

> A sensitive answer turns back wrath,
> but an offensive word stirs up anger. (Proverbs 15:1)

About the Christian Faith

Eating in Peace

Better a little with fear of the LORD
than a great treasure with turmoil.
Better a meal of greens with love
than a plump calf with hate.
(Proverbs 15:16-17)

One year I used this proverb as a responsive reading at our love feast (a full Communion service that includes foot washing and a meal, along with the bread and cup) because it reminds me how important love should be in our gathering in the name of Jesus. One of my religious forebears, Alexander Mack, Jr., wrote an essay in the eighteenth century describing the proper procedure to conduct the love feast, then added that if someone was doing the love feast "wrong," he would make it a point not to mention it because the name of the feast is Love. And that's wisdom too. Sometimes it's better to be good than right. Sometimes it's better to cook up a salad of peace than a feast of contention.

In our modern talking-head culture, rudeness, verbal abuse, insult, and even lies are prized because all that matters is total victory. Yet gentle answers open up the door to reconciliation and peace. I have to remember this every time I think of a stinging response to something that hurts me.

Tried and True

Finally, one of the central concerns of Proverbs is that the lessons learned in the past be passed down to the next generation, helping to ensure the stability and safety of a society founded upon wisdom and the fear of the Lord.

This assumes that wisdom remains valid because human nature stays basically the same from generation to generation. Over the past century, scientific, financial, communication, and social advances have radically changed the assumptions and outlook of succeeding generations.

Consider: Why should one succeeding generation trust the wisdom of the preceding generation? How is trust established from one generation to the next? What trust did you place in those two or three generations before you? How has your wisdom been received by the next generations?

In our own era, new wisdom has developed. Just thinking about the computer age, sayings like "Garbage in, garbage out"; "Don't click send!"; and, of course, "Save early and often" come to mind. In the case of the last one, just about all of us have lost an important computer file because we didn't bother to save before the power went out and we lost our work.

Write your own proverb on the topic of self-control, perhaps taking into account the speed of modern communications or social media. Ask yourself, *Does this proverb provide people with a choice that leads to righteous and good living?*

Live the Story

We owned a primitive video game when our children were young. I allowed our oldest son, Francisco, to play for an hour at a time. Of course, he didn't hesitate to tell us that we were not only awful parents, we were uncool to boot.

I learned to live with that attitude. But everything changed the day Francisco wandered into my writing office and noticed a row of long-playing albums. His mouth dropped, and he was silent for a very long time. Then slowly he pulled the LPs off the shelf as if they were sacred objects. It had not occurred to him that his father listened to the Beatles, the Rolling Stones, and especially Bob Dylan. Maybe Dad knew something after all.

Nowadays all of Cisco's kids are Bob Dylan fans, too; and what little wisdom I had to offer has been passed down. For those who are keeping score, both his sons, Jose and Luis Humberto, have to observe strict time limits when it comes to playing video games. It's nice to know that at least some of what I taught—or my son observed—helped a succeeding generation! Indeed, wisdom helps us live righteously and exercise our freedom in beneficial ways.

What does it take for the generations to make contact? What success have you had in being heard? Which of your rules, maxims, or keys to life have been passed along? Which have not?

1. From http://www.iwise.com/2WQqP. (4-27-11)

3.

If the Shoe Fits . . .

Proverbs 16:1–22:16; 25:1–29:27

Claim Your Story

It's hard not to feel a little smug when you grow up in Los Angeles thinking, *Just another perfect day in paradise.* One of the nicest things was being able to enjoy a morning at the beach in January and then, when it got too hot, drive up into the mountains to play in the snow. Which brings me to Proverbs 25:13:

> Like the coolness of snow on a harvest day
> are reliable messengers to those
> who send them;
> they restore the life of their master.

In warm climates, cooler weather can be found on the hilltops. It's worth a climb to enter a different climate.

We all bring our own perspective to Proverbs. We decide if a particular proverb speaks to us or not. If one doesn't, don't worry. There's another one on the way. And if one applies to us, we can take action. The proverbs put us in life's driver's seat, inviting us to get behind the wheel and take off! (Now there's an LA image, to be sure.)

As you prayerfully read through the Book of Proverbs, one or another proverb may jump off the page and say to you, "This is my life! This is about me!" Some proverbs may even lead you to change your lifestyle. Be prepared to name and claim one or more proverbs as your own.

Enter the Bible Story

These two sections of Proverbs (16:1–22:16; 25:1–29:27), separated from each other in the book, are linked together in this chapter of our study because they have a common purpose and focus: society's order and security. King Solomon's proverbs focus on maintaining the social order, one of the tasks awaiting budding civil servants who were studying Proverbs as part of their training. Wisdom from the great reformer King Hezekiah, who was sometimes called a second Solomon, makes up the second section and focuses on the king's responsibilities regarding the same goal of maintaining the social order.

Revenge Served Warm With Fuzzies

The American Civil War's sesquicentennial occurred in 2011. There were commemorations of glorious actions, but the anniversary also called us to reflect on the atrocities of slavery and the cruel horrors Americans perpetrated on each other.

In that light, it was appropriate that the first Civil War event I attended was one organized by descendants of survivors of the abominable Andersonville prisoner-of-war camp run by the Confederates. The horrific conditions there led to the only war crimes trial connected to the Civil War.

That commemoration came to mind when my eyes landed on Proverbs 25:21-22:

> If your enemies are starving, feed them some bread;
> if they are thirsty, give them water to drink.
> By doing this, you will heap burning coals on their heads,
> and the LORD will reward you.

In ancient warfare, the mistreatment of enemy prisoners was a commonplace. Against that, this bit of wisdom attributed to Solomon suggests doing just the opposite. If you really want to get even with your enemies, kill them with kindness. This counterintuitive advice just might work. It is actually a fairly sophisticated strategy for winning a war. Leaving embittered survivors only plants the seeds for the next war. But long-term peace and stability can result from unexpectedly kind behavior.

This works for churches too. Maybe that's why the apostle Paul quoted this proverb when he wrote, "It is written, . . . *If your enemy is hungry, feed him; if he is thirsty, give him a drink. By doing this, you will pile burning coals of fire upon his head.* Don't be defeated by evil, but defeat evil with good" (Romans 12:19-21), which is not much different from what Jesus said: "Love your enemies" (Matthew 5:44).

Do you see how the biblical proverbs uphold the social order but also gently and subversively turn the world upside down? Warfare was an ever-present reality, but wisdom suggested that there was (and is) also a non-violent alternative.

There are many proverbs that make negative references to the power of the tongue, but there are also those that point to the positive way the tongue can be used to avoid active conflict. For instance, "A commander can be persuaded with patience" (Proverbs 25:15), "Pleasant words are . . . healing to the bones" (16:24), and "Wise are those who restrain their talking" (17:27).

The First Five

Have you ever noticed how an old, well-marked Bible opens up to the previous owner's favorite passage? Where would the Book of Proverbs open?

Remember, Proverbs wasn't really a book originally. It was a scroll. The Mennonite scholar John W. Miller suggested there are 375 proverbs in the central collection of the book, a number divisible by 5, leading him to believe groups studied them 5 at a time. There would be 37 sets of 5 proverbs in the rolled-up scroll in the left hand and 37 sets of 5 proverbs in the rolled-up scroll in the right hand. That left 5 proverbs, the 5 you would see when you first unrolled the scroll:

> All the ways of people are pure in their eyes,
>   but the LORD tests the motives.

> Commit your work to the LORD,
>   and your plans will succeed.
> The LORD made everything for a purpose,
>   even the wicked for an evil day.
> The LORD detests all who are arrogant;
>   they surely won't go unpunished.
> Love and faithfulness reconcile guilt;
>   the fear of the LORD turns away evil.
> (Proverbs 16:2-6)

I don't know if these five are more important than the others, but these five in the middle are the five that the original readers would have seen first. These are the proverbs meant to grab the reader's attention.

Regarding the first one—"All the ways of people are pure in their eyes, / but the LORD tests the motives" (Proverbs 16:2)—I suspect that everyone's ways *are* pure in their own eyes. Isaac Asimov once said that one likely reason his novels were popular was that he had no "bad guys"—none of his characters is a villain in his or her own mind. We may not agree with their motivations, but they all think they're doing the right thing.

In our own dealings it helps to remember that most people don't set out to do wrong. That doesn't mean we don't run into people who are roadblocks, but generally they think they're behaving properly.

What assumptions do you make about others? Do you imagine they know what you are thinking? Reflect on a long-running feud or conflict you have had or are experiencing. What motivates the other person? Do you think the other person understands your motivations?

The Reason for Life's Seasons

The second proverb—"Commit your work to the LORD, / and your plans will succeed" (Proverbs 16:3)—touches another key theme in the book: the value of work. The Hebrew word for work, `asah, has several meanings; but underlying them is the idea that our choice of vocation, our aim in life, is a determining factor in who we are. Work is a central part of our identity. Because for most of us our "work" is also our job, unemployment is not only a financial crisis, it's a spiritual challenge. This is also true when an emotional or physical disability prevents us from doing what we consider our work.

It is just as important to define our identity beyond a job. What is your vocation? What is your passion? What brings you joy? What do you really want to be? Does committing your work to the Lord mean putting your ultimate definition of meaning and accomplishment in God's hands, regardless of the results you observe?

Many times it seems that we're spinning our wheels even when we're working hard. The promise of the proverb is that our plans *will* succeed, eventually. That may not be obvious; but it will happen, even if others finish the job. Our work, if it is God's work, will succeed with us, despite us, or after us. I am reminded of the science writer Willy Ley, a German immigrant who worked tirelessly promoting the idea of space flight in the United States back in the forties and fifties. He worked with filmmakers like Walt Disney and artists like Chesley Bonestell to sell Americans on the idea that travel in space was inevitable. For many years he was like Moses wandering in the desert, but he never lost faith or hope. After the shock of Sputnik, launched by the Soviets in 1957, he had a much more attentive audience in the United States. Alas, also like Moses, he died within sight of the Promised Land, a month before the first moon landing in 1969.

It's All Good

The third proverb—"The LORD made everything for a purpose, / even the wicked for an evil day" (Proverbs 16:4)—addresses a tension we all live with. We see God's purpose in everything, but there's a tension between God's will and our free will. I don't think God wills that some are wicked, that evil exists, that atrocities occur; but this proverb suggests that the ultimate fate of the wicked will fit in with God's overarching plan. It may be that we have more to say about where we fit in that plan than we think. Still, God is actively involved in everything, even if it is unclear to us at this point what God is doing.

Across the Testaments

Like Brother, Like the Son

There's no question that Jesus and his brother James knew Proverbs inside and out. Here are just two examples:

Compare

> Don't exalt yourself in the presence of the king,
>   or stand in the place of important people,
> because it is better that he say to you, "Come up here,"
>   than to be demoted before a ruler. (Proverbs 25:6-7)

with the parable of Jesus in Luke 14:8-11, about taking the place of honor at a wedding before being invited, which ends with the warning, "All who lift themselves up will be brought low, and those who make themselves low will be lifted up."

Compare "Don't brag about tomorrow, / for you don't know what a day will bring" (Proverbs 27:1) with James 4:15: "Here's what you ought to say: 'If the Lord wills, we will live and do this or that.' "

[handwritten margin note: Don't count your chickens before they hatch]

In the meantime, it helps to know that God made everything with a purpose (and that includes mosquitoes, though I remain skeptical). The late Steve Irwin, also known as the Crocodile Hunter, worked tirelessly to educate people around the world about the beauty and value of creatures many dismiss as ugly, vile, dangerous, and dreaded.

True Value

The fourth proverb—"The LORD detests all who are arrogant; / they surely won't go unpunished" (Proverbs 16:5)—reminds us that God is a god of values. God detests the arrogance of those who have put themselves first, who have made gods of themselves. If we truly appreciate the miracle that each human being represents, we cannot afford to be arrogant toward each other. When we engage in debate about Congressional representatives who cut off aid to the mentally disabled and argue about unemployment benefits, when marginalized (and nonvoting!) populations are ignored, it helps to remember that God is actively involved in history, even though it is not clear how things will turn out. The arrogant will have their comeuppance. In the meantime we need to remember that time is on God's side.

Wow!

The final proverb in this group of five—"Love and faithfulness reconcile guilt; / the fear of the LORD turns away evil" (Proverbs 16:6)—reminds us that the universe is founded on love and faithfulness. Moreover, love and faithfulness are not warm fuzzies standing on the sidelines, but active attributes of God that can accomplish the delicate task of reconciliation, especially reconciliation with us. And the thing that can keep us on the straight and narrow is that constant theme in Proverbs, the fear of the Lord. *God gave us a conscience*

Fear of the Lord is not fright. It's getting the big picture, seeing God, seeing God's creation, seeing everything connected together and our place in it, and finding ourselves truly awestruck. The photographs from satellites such as the Hubble Telescope are one way we experience the fear of the Lord in a way that also inspires wonder and love.

When have you had a sense of the presence of God? In what circumstance? How did you react? How long did the experience last? What would life be like if one always felt the awesome presence of God? What would life be like if one never felt it?

Pick five proverbs. Prayerfully reflect on each in turn, relating them to your life of faith. Note your first reactions to each proverb; then delve deeper into the consequences of living God's way, even when immediate benefits are not apparent. Do you have to see a reward immediately to want to follow biblical advice?

The Wisdom of Solomon, the Wisdom of Hezekiah

This chapter's selections from Proverbs include many that have been identified as the wisdom of Solomon. One difference from those we looked at in the previous chapter in this study is that there are far fewer of what are called the antithetical proverbs, those in which two contrasting situations are compared and contrasted.

All gotten wealth

Some themes remain constant. The proverbs teach that while wealth is better than poverty, poverty is a whole lot better than evil, especially injustice, wickedness, greed, and folly. "Better a dry crust with quiet / than a house full of feasting with quarrels" (Proverbs 17:1). "Better to be poor and walk in innocence / than to be on crooked paths and wealthy" (28:6).

The economic component of these proverbs reminds us that there is no divide between our world of devotion and the so-called "real" world. So we read, "Those who close their ears to the cries of the poor / will themselves call out but receive no answer" (Proverbs 21:13). Civil servants who are climbing the rungs of the ladder of power and wealth must never forget that "the rich and the poor have this in common: / the LORD made them both" (22:2).

This selection of Solomonic proverbs focuses often on maintaining social order. So, too, does the Hezekiah section, Proverbs 25:1–29:27, which takes special notice of what a good king, a reforming king, ought to be. Hezekiah of Judah, who reigned in Jerusalem from 715–687 B.C., was the first king since Solomon to have reigned without a competing Israelite king to the north. He was sometimes referred to as a second Solomon (see especially 2 Kings 18:1–20:21; 2 Chronicles 29:1–32:33; and, from the Apocrypha, Sirach 48:17-22).

With the likelihood of invasion by Assyria, the question had to be asked by such a king, "How will we survive?" The answer: Listen to God's Word, the source of wisdom—and not just the wisdom of Proverbs. During the reign of Hezekiah a great many biblical documents were found, collected, and revered, including the history that comprises the books of Joshua, Judges, First and Second Samuel, and First and Second Kings.

Hezekiah was considered that rarity in biblical history, a good king. A good king is open to inquiry. The Department of Research and Development ought never to be underfunded. "It is the glory of kings to discover something" (Proverbs 25:2).

Folly

A good king also avoids folly. The folly and faithlessness of the kingdom of Israel led, in the eyes of those who wrote the biblical histories, to

that part of the world where language, math etc. developed in Eugene

About the Scripture

En Fuego (On Fire)

"Mockers set a city on fire," warns Proverbs 29:8, illustrating the power of rumor and gossip. Literally, the words translated as "mockers" is "men of the tongue." In our television culture, some individuals have no obvious qualifications for success beyond an ability to mock, to tear apart, to tear down. In a 24/7 news cycle that does not allow time for reflection but invites these mockers to parse and pick apart the most obscure events and words, we can certainly—and ruefully—agree with the truth of this proverb.

Israel's destruction at the hands of the Assyrians. That's why folly needs special mention: because folly is avoidable. Yet one gets the impression in Proverbs that people prefer illusion to reality. Fools speak without thinking, act without reflection, know the better way but choose the false path.

Worse than that, folly is contagious. Cascade Theory demonstrates mathematically that left to ourselves, the odds are good we'll get the right answer; but when we're in bad company, we'll be stampeded to share the opinion of fools. One sees this in the hysteria that follows a national trauma. The real danger of World War II led Americans astray in the hysterical act of herding loyal Japanese Americans into detention centers. Americans traumatized (rightfully so) by 9/11 came to believe Iraq was not only the source of terror but also posed a nuclear threat. Sometimes the sky is really falling. Sometimes it's just Chicken Little.

"The mouth of fools is their ruin; / their lips are a trap for their lives" (Proverbs 18:7), we're warned. Civil servants, especially diplomats, know that "it is honorable to back off from a fight"; but alas, "fools jump right in" (20:3).

The Hezekiah portion of Proverbs therefore graphically describes the actions of fools, including the famous, "Like a dog that returns to its vomit, / so a fool repeats foolish mistakes" (Proverbs 26:11). Indeed, the sages knew you can't win for losing. Proverbs 26:4-5 advises the reader not to bother answering fools because you'll just become one but then states you have to answer fools or they'll think they're wise.

We live in a results-oriented society. We want to know what works, and what works right now. The proverbs invite us to take the long view. Considering the traps that tempted kings—as well as modern consumers—the wisdom of Scripture ought, at the very least, help us to maintain our commitment when the rewards of faithfulness are not immediately apparent.

Live the Story

The Scottish poet Robert Burns (1759–1796) is famous for his lyric "Auld Lang Syne." He's also famous for another little poem called "To a Louse. On Seeing One on a Lady's Bonnet, at Church," which should tell you a lot about the poem right there. The key stanza reads:

> O wad some Power the giftie gie us
> To see oursels as ithers see us!
> It wad frae mony a blunder free us,
> An' foolish notion.[1]

Seeing ourselves as others see us—that's an important part of self-knowledge! And that's where the proverbs can help us if we're humble enough to use them like a mirror. It's easy enough to see the way they point out the faults of others. But there's something divine about looking at ourselves from outside, from above.

Hold the mirror of Proverbs up to your own life. Has any proverb jumped out at you—uncomfortably? Have you thought about what it means to make a change in your life by using wisdom instead of by knocking your head against a wall?

1. From http://www.worldburnsclub.com/poems/translations/552.htm. (4-28-11)

4.

True, Reliable Words

Proverbs 22:17–24:34

Claim Your Story

I always liked Farmer Mel, whose photo could appear in the dictionary right next to the term "Old Coot." Mel was an old-school Hoosier farmer who worked until he was well into his nineties. Once he made a bundle by laying out some burlap sacks next to a sign reading, "Pick your own morel mushrooms—$5." Morels go for twenty dollars a pound; but since most people couldn't spot one if they tripped over it, what Mel was really doing was selling old burlap sacks for five bucks apiece.

He also told great stories. My favorite called to mind the proverb "Don't remove an ancient boundary marker / that your ancestors established" (Proverbs 22:28). Mel told about two neighbors who argued about boundary markers that separated their properties. Had an ancestor moved one decades earlier? Hard to say, but both believed that they were being cheated.

According to Mel, they solved their problem by planting a woods only twenty-yards wide along the disputed border. That Peace Forest provided fruit and also rendered their border dispute moot!

What have you learned from the lives of others? What stories from your family or your church do you repeat? Do any demonstrate a wiser way to settle disputes?

Enter the Bible Story

Egypt is like dinosaurs. Sooner or later most kids fall in love with *Tyrannosaurus rex* and King Tut.

Think of the first time you learned about pyramids, pharaohs, mummies, the Nile, agriculture, and the myths. For many kids, history begins with Egypt.

So does wisdom. The proverbs of 22:17–24:34 have roots in ancient Egypt. Some of the Hebrew words in these chapters were difficult to translate until a document from the twelfth century B.C. known as "The Instruction of Amenemope" was published in the first part of the twentieth century. The introduction and the first ten sayings of these "true, reliable words" (22:21) in this portion of Proverbs come directly from Egypt.

Those in the Hebrew court who may have instructed young men preparing for the civil service evidently saw nothing wrong with sharing wisdom rooted in another ancient culture. But then, neither did the other Old Testament writers, some of whom portrayed the Gentile emperors Cyrus and Darius as acting as instruments of God's will.

The same is true for the apostle Paul, who quoted from the comic playwright Menander when he reminded the Corinthians, "Don't be deceived, bad company corrupts good character" (1 Corinthians 15:33). The apostle also quoted from other pagan poets, as when he told the Athenians, "In God we live, move, and exist. As some of your own poets said, 'We are his offspring.' " (Acts 17:28).

The practice continued in the second century when it was common for Christian writers such as Justin Martyr to quote one ancient Greek tragedian after another to prove that the truth about Jesus was foreshadowed in pagan writings.

Despite wisdom's way of intertwining itself among cultures, one still encounters, whether in print or in poorly made documentaries, the claim that if one finds echoes of other cultures in biblical writings, this demonstrates that the Bible is somehow flawed or untrue.

This sort of reasoning is actually what is flawed. God's wisdom does not dwell solely among one small group of people. That's what makes wisdom different from other forms of revelation. There was never any sharp line between biblical and secular wisdom.

Take, for instance, the Golden Rule, known to us through the words of Jesus, "Treat people in the same way that you want them to treat you"

(Luke 6:31). This saying of Jesus is no less true or inspired even though this proverb appeared previously in many different cultures, either in the positive form which is familiar to us ("Do unto others as you would have them do unto you.") or in its negative form ("Do not do unto others as you would not want them to do unto you."). It was also present in Jewish thought at the time of Jesus. It was self-evident and needed no proof.

Good for the Goose, Good for the Gander

The "thirty sayings full of advice and knowledge" with their "true, reliable words" (Proverbs 22:20-21) are mostly written in a strong second-person voice. Some of them were first taught to Egyptian civil servants, before the officials of the Hebrew royal court evidently decided they worked just as well for their own young people. Whether or not this wisdom came directly from God and from God's prophets, it was necessary to memorize these sayings and then enact laws that impacted lives in a positive fashion. It was important that "you have them ready on your lips" (22:18).

One of the real differences between the Hebrew and Egyptian versions is the assurance that the Hebrew God takes the part of the poor. The initial admonition from "The Instruction of Amenemope," "Don't steal from the poor, / because they are poor. / Don't oppress the needy in the gate" (Proverbs 22:22), isn't just a suggestion in the Book of Proverbs. Oppressing the needy would not only result in the Lord taking up their case but would also yield severe and dire consequences for the oppressor: God will "press the life out of those who oppress them" (22:23). This is a startling threat. The word translated as life, *nefesh*, is the word for breath, the gift from God that keeps all of us alive. It is also an indication of how seriously Scripture insists God champions the poor.

This advocacy for the poor and powerless is part of a larger passion for justice in these thirty sayings in particular and in Scripture in general. The question of moving boundary stones, something that was easy to do, is mentioned twice within this section (Proverbs 22:28 and 23:10-11). The latter includes a warning that the redeemer of orphans is both strong and will take action. In the ancient Hebrew society, the redeemer was the family member who made debts good, took charge of social arrangements, and stood up for those who were wronged. The redeemer of the poor, in this context, is none other than the Lord.

What resources for the poor are available in your area? How is your church involved? The poor can be a difficult population to find and serve. Do you or others use anecdotes as an excuse to salve your conscience and ignore the suffering? How should we both serve and require accountability in that service?

Stand Up and Be Counted

This concern for justice also requires standing up for those who are falsely accused, even if it makes one unpopular, especially in capital cases (Proverbs 24:11-12). In our own society, politicians build their careers on capital cases in an effort to appear tough on crime. There are claims that, in some states, evidence that proves a death-row inmate is innocent is suppressed, ignored, or denied so that the machinery of death can proceed. Proverbs suggests we cannot claim innocence in such cases. It is our business to know. Once again referring to the divine redeemer of the weak, the passage warns, "The one who protects your life—he knows. / He makes people pay for their actions" (24:12).

That's why a "rich blessing" (Proverbs 24:25) is promised to those who speak up for the innocent branded guilty by society. That's why

About the Scripture

Call the Court to Order

"Those who say to the guilty, 'You are innocent'—the people will curse them" (Proverbs 24:24). The action of cursing is really a prayer for justice. I ask people who read their Bibles from cover to cover to do the math. Personal salvation is important, and it's what people like to hear about. But justice is mentioned more than salvation, which is an indication of how important God takes it. Blessing and cursing are two sides of the same coin. Listen to wisdom. Do the right thing. Be blessed instead of cursed.

one must not give false witness, even if one has been personally wronged (24:23-26, 28-29). The stability of a society depends on trust in the courts. (By the way, these last sayings, as well as all those included in 24:23-34, are bonus sayings from unnamed sages that the book's compilers thought ought to be added on to the Thirty Sayings of the section.)

How do the courts work in your region? Do people have trust in court cases? What has been the result, in your opinion, of television programs built around real court cases as well as courts established for entertainment purposes? Do you think people in your region have a passion for or a stake in justice?

Common Sense About Cash

Proverbs 23:1-9 refers to table manners. It may seem odd that such a topic is included as wisdom. But the purpose of manners is not to impose an arbitrary set of behaviors that go against the grain, as some suppose, but to equalize social situations between unequals. The social settings described in these nine verses are also a warning against trying to live beyond one's means. (The English humorist Saki parodied this practice a century ago when he had a character say, "All decent people live beyond their incomes nowadays, and those who aren't respectable live beyond other people's means."[1])

The American Revolution was inspired not only by taxation without representation (though that certainly galled the thrifty New Englanders), but by the unwise buying practices of colonial Virginia planters. Typically, these landed gentry sent their tobacco back to Britain, where they got a poor price, and purchased their clothing, furniture, and doodads through their brokers in England, who charged high prices, tacked on high shipping costs, and took a commission. The crop of tobacco depleted the soil, so the yields got smaller. The planters got deeper and deeper in debt and wouldn't change their ways. Thus, Virginians who otherwise had no quarrel with England found themselves uncomfortably in debt to the mother country and therefore more than willing to join the troublesome folks from New England. The New Englanders worried about taxation without

Across the Testaments

Echo

Get your outside work done;
make preparations in the field;
then you can build your house. (Proverbs 24:27)

Sound familiar? It should. As Jesus said, "If one of you wanted to build a tower, wouldn't you first sit down and calculate the cost, to determine whether you have enough money to complete it?" (Luke 14:28). The well-known admonition by Jesus to count well the cost is directed not only to the homebuilder but also to the would-be disciple!

representation and the presence of an occupying army. The Virginia planters were hoping to escape their debts without paying a dime.

Our own buying habits might be described in the humorous two-sentence poem of Proverbs 22:26-27, which warns that if we can't pay back what we borrow, our bed might be foreclosed right underneath us. At the risk of seeming too timely, the credit and housing crises of recent years were partly out of the control of many borrowers; but there were a number of poorly designed lending practices that made things worse.

How do our financial choices affect our ability to live faithful lives of discipleship? Is the financial world separate from the religious sphere? Are your choices in one area of life influenced by your actions in the other? Why, or why not?

The comic image of money growing wings and flying away (Proverbs 23:5) is a staple of modern cartoons; but it has its roots in Egyptian wisdom, confirming what the Teacher of Ecclesiastes means when he says that "there's nothing new under the sun" (Ecclesiastes 1:9).

Spare the Rod—Please!

We're all probably familiar with the proverb "Spare the rod and spoil the child," based on,

> Don't withhold instruction from children;
>   if you strike them with a rod, they won't die.
> Strike them with a rod,
>   and you will save their lives from the grave.
>   (Proverbs 23:13-14)

I grew up in a denomination where it was expected—and even joked about—that our Christian educators would whack us if we didn't behave. I have since left that communion (where that sort of behavior is no longer allowed, of course). Maybe that's why I find this verse so—pardon the expression—striking.

I have heard this saying (along with Proverbs 13:24 and 22:15) quoted any number of times to justify all sorts of ill treatment of children. But this is a good example of how we have to confront and apply wisdom, not just quote it. Most of us would agree that setting limits and applying discipline is an essential part of child rearing, but would we agree about the limits of corporal punishment?

How do we set limits as a society and a church about methods and application of child discipline? To what extent is this proverb helpful? To what extent is it harmful? How have your attitudes changed over the years? How have the attitudes of society and the church changed?

What would Jesus do?

Addictive Behavior

The warnings in Proverbs against addictive behavior can apply to almost everyone. Think back to scandals involving the behavior of celebrities, elected officials, religious leaders, and others in the public eye. Doesn't it make sense that this instruction manual for civil servants would strongly warn about the dangers of wine (Proverbs 23:29-35)? In our time, we would extend that warning to tobacco, alcohol and other drugs, as well as to other dependencies.

Does your congregation have alternatives to wine in Communion or to sweets in a social hour that take into account the addictions with which some people struggle?

The Book of Proverbs often balances humor and realism, as in 23:34-35 where humor is used to illustrate the absurd results of drunkenness. These verses compare the drunkard's staggering to someone on a ship who doesn't have his or her sea legs, but results such as being beaten up without being aware of it are too real for comfort.

Reflect upon your own weaknesses. How did you become aware of your thorn in the flesh? Is your church a help or a hindrance in dealing with it?

Sexual Misconduct

In popular media, those who take a stand against sexual misconduct are often depicted as interfering killjoys who don't want others to have a good time. But the Hebrew Scriptures have a high view of the place of pleasure and sexual fulfillment. The warnings in Proverbs aren't against sexual intercourse. But a strong stand is taken against the weakening of the marriage covenant (Proverbs 23:26-27), with a reminder that prostitution and adultery are not victimless crimes. They weaken society, our health, and our relationships.

How comfortable are you discussing matters of sexuality in an adult Sunday school class or in social settings? What do you think is the boundary regarding the public/private nature of personal behavior?

Sound Foundations

Proverbs upholds the general social order. There is a warning against associating with the rebellious (Proverbs 24:21-22), which must be interpreted in the context of the importance of stabilizing societies that teetered on the edge of chaos every time a ruler died.

It's also worth noting that in other portions of Proverbs, honoring parents is deemed essential. You may recall that of all the Ten Commandments, the injunction to honor one's parents is the only one that includes a reward. There is no guarantee for anyone's individual lifespan, of course. But when there is care for the weakest members of society—the very young, the very old, the infirm, the poor, and others in difficult straits—the society is more secure and safer for all.

Loose Ends

One particularly timely admonition warns against that wonderful German word *schadenfreude*, which means the delight people take in the misfortunes of others:

> When your enemies fall, don't rejoice.
> When they stumble, don't let your heart be glad,
> or the LORD will see it and be displeased,
> and he will turn his anger from them.
> (Proverbs 24:17-18)

There is a gossipy delight when politicians and celebrities fall from grace. There can also be a national animosity toward other countries. Whether animosity is justified or not, this text warns against the toxic nature of this attitude. I am reminded of what Abraham Lincoln said during a particularly dark time in the Civil War. Someone attempted to comfort him by stating that at least God was "on our side." Lincoln would have none of it and replied that the important thing was whether we were on God's side.

Some of the proverbs are poems in praise of wisdom itself. Wisdom is perspective; and although many of us pride ourselves on having graduated from the school of hard knocks, it's OK if we learn from the hard knocks others have taken. It is not necessary for every generation to repeat the same mistakes, although sometimes we are inclined to think that is inevitable.

The warning against laziness (Proverbs 24:30-34) and how lack of wisdom can lead to poverty brings this short collection to a close. This proverb must have spoken directly to the compiler; for he notes, "I observed this and took it to heart; / I saw it and learned a lesson" (24:32).

What lessons have you learned so far from wisdom? Which of these groups of proverbs speak to you most clearly? Which seem to have nothing to do with you? Would someone else agree? What topic that was not covered do you think would have been more helpful to society? To the church? to you?

Live the Story

> Who is suffering? Who is uneasy?
> Who has arguments? Who has complaints?
> Who has unnecessary wounds?
> Who has glazed eyes? (Proverbs 23:29)

Whether you've read Proverbs 23:29-35 or lived it, you'd certainly have to agree that its words are vivid and uncompromising. Wine, we are told, "sparkles in the cup" (23:31) but "bites like a snake" (23:32) and causes us to "see strange things" (23:33). The images of someone who feels no pain when hit, can't remember how he or she got beat up, and can't escape the toxic cycle of addition is probably too familiar to many of us.

Not only did I receive strong warnings about drinking from my father, a very temperate man, I also saw the experiences of others when I went away to college. I could see no connection between the word *party* and those who binge drank until they were reduced to, as we called it, "driving the porcelain bus."

One of the reasons for these proverbs, whether their source is Egyptian, Hebrew, Christian, street smarts, or plain old twenty-first-century cybersmarts, is that we can benefit from the experiences of others who have gone before us. How often have you met people who could quote the Bible, chapter and verse, and yet didn't seem to be able to translate that into the way they lived? How would looking at the experience of other believers have helped them?

In what areas can the experience of other believers help you today? How will you incorporate it?

1. From *The Complete Stories of Saki*, by Hector Hugo Munro (Wordsworth Classics, 1993); page 79.

5.

Words Tried and True

Proverbs 30:1–31:31

Claim Your Story

I suppose we all have our favorite places. Mine is the steep Four-Mile Trail at Yosemite National Park. What I love is that I get dramatic vistas of Half Dome, El Capitan, and several different views of Yosemite Falls, viewed across miles of frightening emptiness. Mystery becomes reality.

For me the words of the sage Agur express the awe and wonder of the big picture I experience in Yosemite:

> Who has gone up to heaven and come down?
> Who has gathered the wind by the handful?
> Who has bound up the waters in a garment?
> Who has established all the ends of the earth?
> (Proverbs 30:4)

For me the hike usually ends at Glacier Point (7,200 feet), and I still don't have answers to the profound questions. But these last two chapters of Proverbs aren't meant for that. Instead, the words from Agur the sage, the words from the mother of King Lemuel, and the words about the competent household manager together provide me with advice for the little moments. Confronted with the awe and wonder of the big picture, that'll have to be enough.

Perhaps it will be enough for you, too, when you contemplate the big picture of the world God has given us.

Enter the Bible Story

You may have heard the proverb, "Save the best for last." That's the opposite of what was usually done at first-century weddings in Cana in Galilee. When Jesus changed water into wine at such an occasion (John 2:1-11), the headwaiter noted to the groom, "Everyone serves the good wine first" (2:10a). But after tasting the wine Jesus had created, the headwaiter was surprised and said, "You kept the good wine until now" (2:10c). That's just one example of how a great proverb doesn't suit every occasion. When it comes to wisdom, biblical or otherwise, it's up to us to use our own good sense to determine if a proverb fits a particular situation.

We've come to the end of the Book of Proverbs. Has the compiler saved the best for last so that the collection ends with a bang? Or did he follow the headwaiter's expectation that the palate would be dulled, either by too much wine or too many proverbs, and so has served up the best first?

That's up to you to decide. Either way, whoever edited this collection chose these last proverbs as the last things to be read. Who would that have been? It may have been Agur, Jakeh's son, whose proverbs comprise all of Proverbs 30. Was he the court official appointed by Hezekiah to knock Proverbs into shape? In that case, he meant for his words to be the apex, the climax of the book.

His proverbs are followed by a section that many consider an appendix, added later. These include the words of King Lemuel's mother and a description of a "competent wife."

So, Who Are You Anyway?

Agur's identity is a mystery. The text tells us simply that he is "Jakeh's son, from Massa" (Proverbs 30:1). Some scholars suggest the location, Massa, means he was not an Israelite. Agur's name might mean "assembler"; and his father's name, which appears nowhere else, could mean "obedient." This might suggest he was a foreign-born official who had important religious duties in Israel. Massa can also be translated "oracle," an appropriate word to be associated with one who passes along wisdom;

About the Scripture

Out of Gas

Agur's opening words, translated as "I'm tired, God" (Proverbs 30:1), have been interpreted by some to mean he is either an agnostic who states that humans can have no knowledge of God or an atheist who says bluntly that there is no God. But his words suggest that even though there is much that is essentially unknowable about God (30:4), we can learn something of God through the revealed word (30:5-6), by observing the natural world and humanity, and by experience. Life remains full of mystery, but it also taught Agur truths that we can benefit from as well. If we take those truths seriously, they may prevent us from having to devote an entire life learning them for ourselves in the school of hard knocks.

and the name Agur might also be translated as "sojourner," a reminder that we're all just passing through this world.

Perhaps all these meanings were meant to come into play. It could be that Agur was aware of these ambiguities and deliberately embraced the uncertainty.

If so, and if Agur is a wise, obedient assembler who's just passing through, it's no surprise that he has grown weary in service. In words that are difficult to translate, he notes, "I'm tired, God; / I'm tired, God, and I'm exhausted" (Proverbs 30:1). This statement certainly anticipates the Book of Ecclesiastes, which was probably written centuries later. One thing's for sure: Agur's not telling the truth when he continues by writing, "I'm too stupid to be human, / a man without understanding" (30:2) and goes on to say that he hasn't "learned wisdom" (30:3). These self-deprecating remarks mask the fact that his brilliant words reveal a writer who is not only a perceptive observer of human nature but also a masterful poet.

His first poem (in Proverbs 30:4), asking who truly understands Creation, calls to mind God's demanding answer to Job at the climax of that book (Job 38–41). Agur's previous admission that he is "a man without understanding" actually displays a good deal of understanding and wisdom because the more you know, the more you know you don't know! Certainly our scientific inquiries have only increased our sense of awe and mystery.

By asking the rhetorical question, "Who has gone up to heaven and come down?" (Proverbs 30:4), Agur warns all of us, especially those of us who might consider ourselves expert in God's Word, to approach the task of interpretation with humility. Yet how often do we hear the overconfident words of a preacher who claims to know exactly what a Scripture passage means, to the exclusion of all other interpretations, especially when it comes to predicting the end of the world? "Scripture is clear!" the preacher proclaims triumphantly; and though over the centuries others have foundered over the passage, this individual *knows*.

But faith is not faith if we really know everything. No matter how assured we feel, no matter how close our relationship to the Savior, true faith requires a leap in the dark. The wise ones thousands of years ago faced up to the awesome mysteries of birth, death, and the fact that the awe-inspiring universe exists—and so do we! Their response, and ours, is to stay the course; serve up meals (for ourselves and for the poor); birth babies; cherish loved ones; and live fully in the present, with the assurance that when our time is past, the cosmos will not pass away.

In C. S. Lewis' novel *Till We Have Faces*, a character who has experienced inexplicable suffering finds the will to endure, noting that sometimes God does not give an answer; sometimes God *is* the answer.

Can you think of a sermon you've heard, whether in person or on television, in which the preacher seemed to know everything, and to know that everyone else has been wrong? Have you ever felt trapped, or even battered, by someone's apparent biblical knowledge? What gives you the strength to endure?

Keeping Score

The next poem (Proverbs 30:5-6) describes the words of God in terms that remind us of Psalm 46:1: "God is our refuge and strength." Agur then alludes to the instructions of Deuteronomy 4:2 and 12:32 (and anticipates the closing words of Revelation [22:18-19]!) where we are told to neither add nor take away from God's Word.

Agur next uses the by-now familiar "counting proverb" literary practice to list self-evident truths. Some are grim, as when the consuming grief

A Prayer Behind the Prayer

It's impossible to say if Agur's prayer in Proverbs 30:7-9 had any influence on Jesus when he taught the Lord's Prayer to his disciples, but Jesus' unique prayer pleads for daily bread because that leads us away from temptation. Agur asks to be delivered from poverty because otherwise he might dishonor God by stealing. But Agur realizes that the other extreme (riches) can also be a trap because if he is too satisfied, he will no longer recognize God as our Father. Also, by asking, "Who is the LORD?" he won't be proclaiming "the holiness of [God's] name" (as Jesus did in the Lord's Prayer [Matthew 6:9]).

of infertility is counted with the heartlessly devouring trio grave, water, and fire (Proverbs 30:15-16). Some are thoughtful, as when the walks of a lion, a rooster, and a male goat—three creatures at quite different places in the food chain—are compared to the strut of the king (30:29-31). Some are just common sense, as in the reminder that "stirring up anger produces strife" is a natural process as surely as "churning milk makes curds" and "squeezing the nose brings blood" (30:32-33).

One of the wittiest sections—and most perceptive—includes observations that prove his premise that "four things are among the smallest on earth, / but they are extremely wise": ants, badgers, locusts, and lizards. Though small, they each demonstrate strength in a different way (Proverbs 30:24-28).

Do you enjoy documentaries about the natural world? Do you live in a place where you can observe nature easily? What wisdom have you learned from creation? What insights, if any, into human nature have been revealed to you? What is the nature of your respect, or lack of it, for God's creation?

A Firm Foundation

Agur's greatest scorn is for those who reject the social order (Proverbs 30:21-23), especially when it comes to the commandment in Exodus 20:12 and Deuteronomy 5:16 about honoring one's parents (Proverbs 30:11-14, 17). Though some translations try to blunt the earthy edge of Hebrew poetry, Agur says that those who abuse their parents and engage in other behaviors that are toxic to society "haven't washed off their own excrement" (30:12).

Our society sometimes confuses lack of responsibility and accountability with freedom. One hears that the Bible is full of "Thou shalt nots" that take the fun from life and hem people in. No wonder some people don't want to come to church. But Agur's urgent respect for God's commandments is grounded in the recognition that God's laws are not restrictions or limitations. These boundaries actually provide the freedom for authentic and secure life. The Word of God brings the hope and security God promised to the people. The alternatives to boundaries are not freedom, but anarchy and chaos. Have you ever noticed that whenever there is a breakdown of the social order in a nation during a war or after a natural disaster, the result is not the creation of a utopia, but hell on earth?

We may not agree with some of the examples Agur uses, such as his disdain when a servant becomes a king or a female servant replaces her mistress (Proverbs 30:22-23). In the latter case, Agur is likely using the biblical story of Hagar and Sarah (Genesis 16:1-6) to suggest that people need to remain in their social place to ensure stability and peace. Though we would feel more comfortable than Agur with either of these rags-to-riches scenarios, it is only because we have created new political boundaries, such as those contained in the Bill of Rights, that help to ensure stability.

Name some of the changes you have observed in society in your lifetime. Which have been beneficial? Which, in your opinion, have been no improvement at all? Which have been harmful?

Why Do Fools Fall in Love?

Perhaps the most beautiful and thoughtful mystery probed by Agur involves the four things he can't figure out (Proverbs 30:18-19). These include the aching sense of beauty that comes from watching an eagle soar, the shiver that accompanies the movement of a snake, the bravery of a ship daring the forces of chaos on the open sea, and "the way of a man with a young woman." (Or, as the golden oldie asks, "Why do fools fall in love?") This may be one of the most profound observations in all of Scripture; for what is involved is not only individual happiness, but the well-being of society and the propagation of the human race.

This is why, in my opinion, wedding services are very important. I don't think there is any magic or mysterious operation that takes place that only a minister can accomplish by leading a couple through their vows. Indeed, I would almost agree with those who say that they don't need a piece of paper to live in love. But the covenant of marriage is made not only between two people but also with God and humanity. We're all involved in a marriage. Our social well-being and the care for children, for each other, and for the generations all benefit from it.

The Bible's celebration of human sexuality is best displayed in Song of Songs. Agur, by contrast, provides a striking image of just how ugly and how utterly unmysterious our sexual life becomes when we separate ourselves from proper employment and enjoyment of it. So he writes,

> This is the way of an adulterous woman:
>   she eats and wipes her mouth,
>   and she says, "I've done nothing wrong!"
>   (Proverbs 30:20)

How did your romantic relationships begin? What did others think about them? What blessings—or what harm— have come through these relationships?

Moms Know Best

The short section titled "Words of King Lemuel" (Proverbs 31:1-9) actually consists of the words of his mother. He, too, may be from Massa; or these words may also be oracles, or both. Mom's advice begins with the word that children grow very familiar with: "No, no, no!" And the advice is extremely important: Just because you *can* doesn't mean you *should*.

A king can be a symbol of absolute freedom in the worst sense. Lemuel's mother insists that "wine, women, and song" (to use the common phrase) are not the keys to happiness, nor do they make for a good king.

Kings must never "violate the rights of the needy" (Proverbs 31:5) because it is their duty to "speak out on behalf of the voiceless… / and to defend the needy and the poor" (31:8-9).

I'm reminded once more of C. S. Lewis, in this case the novel *The Horse and His Boy*, one of the Chronicles of Narnia. In this book, a young man named Shasta discovers that he is not an orphan but the son of a king and destined to become king himself. His newfound father explains that being a king means being first in every charge; last in every retreat; and in times of famine, setting an example by tightening his belt and refusing to complain. Social responsibility, not personal appetite, must govern his choices.

In our society, we sometimes see the rich, the powerful, and the famous making poor decisions because there is no one brave enough to tell them no. Lemuel is blessed with a mom whose precepts, far from creating nagging restrictions, give him the tools to succeed.

Whom do you trust to tell you no? Do you listen? When has it been necessary for you to speak prophetically to another, to encourage him or her to make better choices? When you first experienced adult "freedom," did you take it to excess? Did anyone provide a check or balance to your behavior? What place does the church have in prayerfully intervening? What is your level of resentment toward anyone who might intrude into what you consider your "private" life?

Keeping It All in Order

The final portion of Proverbs has been criticized in the past because it seemed to some that it hemmed in women by creating an ideal of one chained to household chores. But this image of the "competent wife" is based on the ancient household, in which rich women had control of finances and the family business. Women like Susanna, Joanna, and Mary Magdalene (Luke 8:1-3), who financially supported the ministry of Jesus, are similar examples of competence and success. One also finds home-owning women like Lydia (Acts 16:40), as well as the sisters Mary and Martha (Luke 10:38-40), who provided both hospitality and charitable works for the community of God.

Throughout history, women have played a central role in the economy of the household. These women are not always rich, but they put their families first. It's for this reason that women receive the vast majority of all microloans distributed in the Third World. They start businesses and bring in money for their children. I wonder if our view of a woman's "proper place" in society has been infected by an image of a sort of golden age that probably never really existed?

Live the Story

As we close our study of Proverbs, it becomes clear that these nuggets of wisdom do not solve any of life's great mysteries. But they give us the tools to live authentically, according to the will of the Creator, whose hand in history is sometimes unseen but whose guidance is sure.

I have to say that the insights I learned during my three years in seminary have served me well over the three decades thus far of my ministry. Still, the best lessons I learned occurred during my first pastorate in a multiracial church in Los Angeles. The membership included two retired African American preachers who had come up through the ranks the hard way. They both were kind enough to teach me what I really needed to know about human nature, urban ministry, and active caring. I learned when to say yes and when to say no, how to be present in the midst of busy lives, and how to be the hands of Jesus in a multicultural setting.

Some people think the only way we can learn for ourselves is by making the same mistakes others have made. I like to believe that we can learn from the wisdom of others.

Likewise, faith is not a matter of certainty but of accepting the mystery of God and doing the work at hand as best we can with what we have learned from people whose wisdom we respect.

What have you had to learn for yourself? Could you have learned it from others? Do you resent what others teach you? Have you ached to help others avoid mistakes similar to those you've made? What attitude do you need to have to be able to benefit from the experience of others?

6.

Been There. Done That. Bought the T-Shirt.

Ecclesiastes 1:1–6:12

Claim Your Story

I helped operate a nursery school back in Los Angeles a couple of decades ago. Some mornings on my way into my office, I stopped for a few moments to watch the kids play. *How wonderful*, I'd think. *So carefree. No worries. It must be great to be a kid.*

Then suddenly one day when all the kids were on their knees, drawing on the pavement with colored chalk, one little girl suddenly stood up with arms outstretched and yelled, "We're all going to die!"

I have no idea where that came from. Was she quoting some movie or TV show? Did she suddenly realize that we're all mortal? No matter. None of the other kids looked up from their artwork. The little girl bent over and rejoined them. Everything returned to normal.

How old were you when you first realized that everything dies and you are going to die? What was your reaction? What is life like for you on your worst days? Do you feel free to express it when you're feeling down? Or do you hide it? Is a struggle with sadness part of your Christian experience?

Enter the Bible Story

There's something about family camp. Everyone is roughing it together outdoors—swimming; hiking; eating real food; enduring mosquito bites; and then, at night, listening to scary stories around the campfire.

The Jewish festival of Sukkot, the Feast of Tabernacles or Tents, was a lot like family camp. Everyone left town to spend time in tents for several days. There was a lot of real food; fresh fruit and vegetables from the just-finished harvest; along with games, fellowship, and fun. The festival had a serious purpose, however: to remind the people of the years they or their ancestors spent in the desert so that they would not take home and land for granted.

Whether or not they gathered around a campfire at night, there was one scary story they told during the festival: the Book of Ecclesiastes! Each year it was read aloud to the people who had returned to the tents.

Ecclesiastes is unlike anything else in Scripture. It can seem grim at times and very pessimistic. It seems to suggest that there are no clear answers to some of life's tough questions. The writer even appears to question whether life has any meaning.

So, what is this book doing as part of a festival of joy?

What is this book doing in your Bible?

What does it mean for your life and faith as a person of the Word?

Good Question

You wouldn't be the first one to ask these questions. According to the venerable Rabbi Akiba, who died in A.D. 135, there were those who questioned whether Ecclesiastes should be a part of the Scriptures.

But it is.

Some of the ancient rabbis, accepting Solomon as the author, explained away the difficulties by suggesting that the king famed for his wisdom wrote Song of Songs first, when he was young; then Proverbs, when he was mature; and finally Ecclesiastes, when he had grown old, tired, and bitter. But most experts agree that Solomon did not write the book. It's true that at one point the writer says that he is the king who is the son of David (Ecclesiastes 1:1), which would suggest, well, Solomon. However, that seems to be a mask so he can engage in a thought experiment—the man who has everything and enjoys nothing. Within a few chapters the author reveals that he is part of the court, not the king, because he has to deal with the frustrations of inflexible bureaucracies.

So who is he? The opening verse tells us the author is "the Teacher of the Assembly" (Ecclesiastes 1:1). The underlying Hebrew word, *qoheleth*, refers to a speaker in the midst of the people. Nothing more is known about who the Teacher might be. But more important than the question of who wrote Ecclesiastes is why it was written.

One answer might be that since, at least part of the time, some of us look at the world as the Teacher did, we need to hear this. We need to listen—and talk back! The wisdom of the Old Testament is part of an ongoing conversation, and we're expected to take part. That's how Wisdom Literature works. We are not meant to be passive receivers. Listen carefully to what the Teacher has to say, and then respond.

Talk It Out

Conversation is essential to Bible study. That was true for the Hebrew believers for thousands of years. It was true for Jesus. We witness this sort of debate in the Gospels. We also witness Paul and the other apostles in dialogue in the Book of Acts. Even Paul's letters are conversational in nature, though we hear only his half of the talking. It is true for us as well when we meet for group Bible study.

The viewpoint of the Teacher is essential to a healthy church—as long as it is not the only voice. Just as we need to grasp Joel's uplifting vision when everyone is filled with God's Spirit, so also we need to acknowledge the bleak outlook of Ecclesiastes when we're in a dark night of the soul. Likewise, the local church board must include both dreamers and realists.

Ecclesiastes is of no use to anyone who believes in what I call a One-Verse Bible. Perhaps you have met the sort of person who has one verse he or she quotes to the exclusion of all others; it is that person's answer to anything troubling that someone might say. That single verse taken out of context is supposed to fit every situation.

As a pastor, I've had people tell me, "I'm really hurt. I'm really suffering. But I shouldn't tell God about it." Ignoring for a moment the fact that God already knows what we're thinking, I would offer the Book of Ecclesiastes as a response to this attitude. The Teacher's monologue is the sort of thing that many people think is not very religious; but he asks the tough questions about pain, suffering, doubt, injustice, and meaninglessness.

One thing is certain: This austere book contains some of the most startling and beautiful poetry ever written. It is a literary masterpiece, appreciated by believers and nonbelievers alike.

On those occasions when I have led study groups through the Bible in a year, many people found this book beautiful, even inspiring, despite its difficult nature. I'll never forget the response of one woman who lived a very hard life. Her children were difficult to deal with. Her husband wasn't much help. There was never enough money. I wondered if Ecclesiastes would depress her, but she told me she couldn't put Ecclesiastes down. She was a woman of great faith who believed God was actively involved in her life, and her faith was evident in the way she lived. She thought Ecclesiastes was the most beautiful biblical book she'd ever read because it told her that someone else had experienced a difficult life like hers and hadn't given up.

And that's the point, isn't it? Life can be confusing and uncertain. Yet that doesn't stop us, as people of faith, from continuing to live lives of faithfulness.

The Story So Far

Ecclesiastes has no story line, no plot development. It may have been one of the last books of the Hebrew Scriptures to be written. Its language suggests it was written in the third century B.C. Its reference to runners and racing suggests Jews had come in contact with the Greek culture of athletics, a relatively late development in the Old Testament period.

The author begins with the harsh statement that life is pointless. Yet despite this grim outlook, he insists on living a religious life. In the end, he decides the antidote to despair is in those things that bring joy, even though he knows they won't last.

The Teacher doesn't despair. He goes on.

Other voices in the Bible disagree with his viewpoint. According to the Teacher, the sun "returns panting to the place where it dawns"

About the Scripture

Breath . . .

The Hebrew word *hevel*, which is nicely translated as "perfectly pointless" (Ecclesiastes 1:2) in the Common English Bible, occurs thirty-eight times in Ecclesiastes. It is a breath of a word—literally. The image it calls up is of a vapor, something that departs so quickly you may not even be aware of it before it passes. The word can be understood to mean futile, ephemeral, incomprehensible, absurd, senseless, and vain. This opening phrase of Ecclesiastes has been translated in many ways, including, "futility, utter futility"; "a vapor of vapors!"; "emptiness, emptiness"; "nothing is worthwhile"; "utterly vain, utterly vain"; "Meaningless! Meaningless!"; and, of course, "Vanity of vanities."

(Ecclesiastes 1:5). We have the image of a weary sun huffing and puffing with exhaustion. Contrast this with the viewpoint of Psalm 19:5:

> The sun is like a groom
>   coming out of his honeymoon suite;
> like a warrior,
>   it thrills at running its course.

What a startling difference! Both the psalmist and the Teacher are looking at the same sun, but each one's view of it is influenced by his or her personal outlook.

That doesn't mean either is wrong. There are days when it feels like everything's coming up roses. There are other days when we know just what Judith Viorst meant when she titled a children's book *Alexander and the Terrible, Horrible, No Good, Very Bad Day.*

So let's listen. Let's talk with and talk back to the Teacher, who is one of the greatest writers who ever lived.

An Answer in Joy

The first eleven verses set out the Teacher's main argument, that nothing really matters. Why does he believe that everything is "perfectly pointless" (Ecclesiastes 1:2)? He believes this because no matter how hard we work, our work will be forgotten. Rivers flow to the sea, but the ocean never fills up. Winds blow round and round. Generations come and go, but "there's nothing new under the sun" (1:9).

When we think about bare tombstones, their writing worn away by the wind and weather after only ten or twelve decades, lying untended in a weed-filled graveyard, or about the massive amount of personal digital data that becomes inaccessible every time there's an advance in technology, it's hard not to agree with the Teacher when he says, "There's no remembrance of things in the past.... Neither will there be any remembrance among those who come along in the future" (Ecclesiastes 1:11).

Beyond those opening verses, the Teacher cuts to the heart of the real question that troubles many, one of being and nonbeing:

> All go to the same place:
> all are from the dust;
> all return to the dust. (Ecclesiastes 3:20)

(Do you remember the once-popular bumper sticker, "The one who dies with the most toys wins"? I recently spotted a grimmer one: "The one who dies with the most toys still dies.")

It's true that the billions of ordinary people over the centuries who have lived and loved and endured and triumphed or failed—and have died—are no longer known to us. Each is known to and is dear to God, of course; but the Teacher insists that among humans, individuals are eventually forgotten.

I'd like to argue that with the Teacher, however. Consider, for example, the Anasazi, who lived a thousand years ago in the American Southwest. You would think the individual identities of the Anasazi would be lost forever. Though they built magnificent structures that were unmatched until the late nineteenth century and endured for centuries in a harsh and unforgiving climate, they left no written records. Only the ruins of their cliff dwellings, as well as their garbage pits and their art, remain. Yet much is known about their ordinary lives. Dendrochronology, for instance, the study of tree rings, makes it possible for scientists to date the construction of individual rooms in a building to within a year or so. Thanks to forensics, a bone, a skull, or a few teeth can tell a scientist the gender, the health, the size, the length of life, of individuals and how they died. Their teeth reveal their age during years of famine and plenty. Indeed, in the cases of many, health histories and life stories can be developed for each individual—everything but a name! The Teacher is wrong, I think. They may have returned to the dust, but there is a great deal of remembrance of things past.

The Teacher gives his own answer in the face of a lost past, lost health, lost wealth, and lost remembrance: The one thing that has value is joy. "There's nothing better for human beings than to eat, drink, and experience pleasure in their hard work" (Ecclesiastes 2:24). He will enjoy what is good while he can, even if that enjoyment, too, fails him. These pleasures are "God's gift. Indeed, people shouldn't brood too much over the days of their lives because God gives an answer in their hearts' joy" (5:19-20).

Are our days truly nothing but "pain, and . . . aggravation" (Ecclesiastes 2:23)? We might feel that way some of the time; but ask yourself, Haven't there been good days, too?

Perfectly Normal

I want to lift up two very positive passages. In the first, the Teacher emphasizes how important companionship is for mutual care and support. He gives several reasons why two people are better off together than one alone and why three is even better (see Ecclesiastes 4:9-12). Friendship, companionship, and fellowship are essential!

But the passage that people probably know best from this book is the famous poem about time in Ecclesiastes 3:1-8 that begins, "There's a season for everything / and a time for every matter under the heavens." (You've probably heard the popular song written by folk singer Pete Seeger, which basically sets the King James translation of this passage to music.)

Across the Testaments

Check Your Clock

The famous poem about time in Ecclesiastes 3:1-8 reminds us there is a time for everything, a time not determined by the ticking of the clock, but by the approach of a season of life. In the New Testament, there are two different words for time. *Kronos* refers to chronological clock time (as in Acts 7:17: "When it was time for God to keep the promise he made"); *kairos* (as in Revelation 1:3: "The time is near") is much closer to the Old Testament concept. Like the concept of time in Ecclesiastes, the meaning of *kairos* is that a season is upon us, not that the game clock is running out.

Beginning with a time for birth and a time for death, the poem simply names opposite pairs of experiences. Each of these is to be understood as perfectly normal. Half of them are obviously more pleasant, and the other half might make you miserable; but the point is that there's nothing wrong with our experiences.

I remember when one of my aunts complained to my mother that everybody was dying and the world was terrible. Mom reminded her that when they were younger, everyone they knew was also younger. In those days, everyone they knew was giving birth. Now time's stream had simply taken them to the place where it was normal for their contemporaries to go about the business of dying. Nothing was wrong. Everything was perfectly normal.

For centuries, Ecclesiastes has provided inspiration to artists. The short story "A Rose for Ecclesiastes," by Roger Zelazny, was published in 1963 (only months before Mariner 4 was launched on November 28, 1964) and demolished the myth of Mars as the home of a dying civilization. It is about a minister's son who, despite having lost his faith, brings Ecclesiastes, and hope, to the Martians, who have accepted the word of their prophets that it was time for their ancient culture to die. After translating Ecclesiastes into Martian, he tells them that even though his own people heard these words, they refused to give up. They chose life.

Something keeps us going even when life seems to have no meaning. One of the most powerful interviews I ever heard involved Dr. Clea Koff, sometimes referred to as the Bone Woman. She had decided as a child that she wanted to become a forensic anthropologist. Her work took her to the sites of many mass murders, where the victims of genocide had been hastily buried. Her job was to give people names again by restoring their identities through her forensic work. One of the things that amazed her was the response of the survivors. Despite being witnesses to events that should have taken away all hope, they seem to have decided that survival was the best revenge. Faced with injustice and despair, they had babies. Though nothing could erase the memories of the horrors they had endured, they knew their children would grow up with no knowledge of what had occurred; and that gave them hope.

Perhaps this is the answer that the Teacher expected his teachings to elicit. Perhaps this example tells us how we should respond: by going on.

The Teacher seems to believe that things don't change. What changes have you observed in society, in your family, and in your church?

Not counting the poem about time (Ecclesiastes 3:1-8), have you heard many—or any—sermons about Ecclesiastes? If you have, how did they affect your life of faith?

Live the Story

My hands shook as I knelt by the shore of my favorite river with the little bag of ashes that were all that remained of my good friend, a little beagle named Krispyn. I wanted to say something profound or poetic, but my throat tightened.

Instead, I thought about how the little puppy craned her neck to get the most beagle bay per buck. I thought about the time I was exhausted— the coldest night of the year—and I was looking forward to eating a sandwich I'd left on a high shelf. But when my back was turned, Krispyn had leaped higher than I could imagine and stolen the sandwich, eating everything but the jalapeños. I thought of how we seemed to read each other's thoughts.

Finally, I shook her ashes into the same river where I plan for my own ashes to be spread.

The Teacher says, "Who knows if a human being's life-breath rises upward while an animal's life-breath descends into the earth?" (Ecclesiastes 3:21). I sure don't have an answer, but my life has been blessed by the courage of my animal friends and my faith in God. So I'll just muddle forward and trust in God's goodness.

In the end, it's what we believers do.

7.

Nothing's Forever, and Everything's Eternal

Ecclesiastes 7:1–12:14

Claim Your Story

My daughter-in-law Margaret Ramirez, who was born in Costa Rica, knows lots of sayings I'd never heard before she mentioned them. One she learned as a child goes like this: *No hay mal que dure cien años ni cuerpo que lo resista o aguante*, which essentially means, "There isn't any evil that lasts a century, nor will anybody have to endure anything that long either." In other words, nothing lasts forever. This too shall pass. Thank heavens. Bad stuff, good stuff, and all the stuff in between comes to an end sooner or later. Pain is real. Injustice is real. Life is not always a picnic. But that doesn't mean the people love life any less. Awareness of life's brevity helps some to live it with zest.

The author of Ecclesiastes has seen it all, has done it all, and has come to the same conclusion. His response: Serve God and live well because nothing lasts forever.

Is there a saying or a bit of folk wisdom you have received from others or that you share during rough moments that gives perspective on good days and bad? How comforting do you find such sayings?

Enter the Bible Story

Pastors serve more than just the members of their church. One night I had a call to visit a young couple I scarcely knew at the hospital. The wife had gone into labor far too early, and the tiny infant had died before he was born. I sat with the mother and father as a kind nurse brought them the little body, and we sat together for a while. We shared a time of baptism and prayer. Although I can't remember my exact words—there aren't any scripts for times like this—I spoke about how they would never forget the child's name, that he was loved, and how he would continue to live in their hearts as well as with God. For those reasons, his life had meaning and purpose.

Life went on. We kept in touch. Babies followed. Still, that little one wasn't forgotten, nor was our wish that he could have had a longer life and the pleasure of all that life has to offer.

Having said this, I have to wonder what the Teacher of Ecclesiastes (1:1) meant when he said that a stillborn child is better off than a discontented person (6:3) "because that child arrives pointlessly, then passes away in darkness. Darkness covers its name" (6:4). Is he right when he says such a child has "more peace than those who live a thousand years twice over but don't enjoy life's good things" (6:5-6)? Sorry, but I have to argue with this Scripture. The memory of that young couple still brings a tear to my eye. The Teacher's words make me uncomfortable. But the Teacher wants us to take a good, hard look at death and life and think about purpose and meaninglessness. He's already told us that life is "perfectly pointless" (1:2). This second half of Ecclesiastes certainly forces us to confront death. The real question is, How will we respond?

How Is It Better?

I often read Ecclesiastes 7:1-2 at funerals. The first part, "A good name is better than fine oil," seems to make good sense; but the second seems totally unrelated. How is "the day of death better than the birthday"? Typically, in Hebrew poetry, when two parallel statements are made, the second echoes the first. In this case, the value of a good name seems obvious; but how is that related to the odd statement about the day of death?

Well, at funerals I remind people that there is no question that the day of birth is a day of joy, when potential for the newborn is unlimited. What about the day of death? Though filled with tears, it is also the day when we know if that potential was fulfilled. We know how the life was lived; how it was ended; and if, indeed, the bearer has a good name that can never be tarnished.

This explanation makes it clear why each saying in Ecclesiastes needs to be discussed and mined for its meaning by people studying their Bibles together.

Simply spouting a series of sayings doesn't make us wise. In the play *Hamlet* the character Polonius reels off a series of proverbs for the benefit of his son Laertes ("Clothes make the man," "Neither a borrower nor a lender be," "To thine own self be true."[1]), none of which we can argue with; but he ends up looking like a fool. We, too, look foolish if all we do is give advice and never listen.

The Teacher also says, "Don't ask, 'How is it that the former days were better than these?' / because it isn't wise to ask this" (Ecclesiastes 7:10). I take issue with this as well. I don't know why people assume the past was automatically better. Would you really wish to live in an age before antibiotics? At the risk of sounding heretical, I have to laugh when I hear people say they wish they could have lived in pioneer days, especially after they've watched a few episodes of *Little House on the Prairie*. That show taught wonderful lessons but in truth ought to have been titled *Little Drudge on the Prairie*.

On the Other Hand

But sometimes I agree with Ecclesiastes. The Teacher makes one of his most profound observations when he tells us life isn't fair! The good die too soon. Wicked people don't seem to get their comeuppance (see Ecclesiastes 7:15). Not only that, "the race doesn't always go to the swift, nor the battle to the mighty, nor food to the wise, nor wealth to the intelligent, nor favor to the knowledgeable" (9:11).

Sometimes the only honest answer is, "I don't know." That's the answer the Teacher gives when he admits that wisdom fails him and that he can't get to the bottom of some mysteries (see Ecclesiastes 7:23-25).

Wisdom truly fails the Teacher when he makes profoundly mistaken comments about women. Having found one woman "more bitter than death: she who is a trap, her heart a snare, her hands shackles" (Ecclesiastes 7:26), he concludes that if a good man is one in a thousand, "I couldn't find a woman among any of these" (7:28). I call this the "devil with the blue dress on" argument, one that fails to convince. Adam was the first to use it when he said, "The woman you gave me, she gave me some fruit from the tree, and I ate" (Genesis 3:12). Adam, like the Teacher, fails to take his share of the blame.

For that matter, why are women blamed for the feelings and attitudes that some men project onto them?

Once again, if we believed in a One-Verse Bible, this statement taken by itself and quoted out of context could be used to marginalize all women. But the Teacher, who is not worried about consistency, reverses himself and later says, "Enjoy life with your dearly loved spouse" (Ecclesiastes 9:9); and one must assume that this is a positive statement about women.

Fortunately, few, male or female, share his exasperating viewpoint about women. However, any man or woman who has been badly wronged, is newly divorced, or is suffering in a difficult relationship might make negative generalizations about the opposite sex. Indeed, a witty comedian, female or male, can make us all laugh with generalizations about the other gender. Gentle, not biting, humor can give us all better perspective and can enable us to laugh at what is silly in ourselves. But the Teacher's bitter comments on women in this context are not helpful.

Then There's This One

This isn't the only topic on which the Teacher contradicts himself. On the one hand, he warns us to be quick to leave the presence of the king. "Don't linger in a harmful situation / because he can do whatever he wants!" (Ecclesiastes 8:3). Then again, "If a ruler's temper rises against you, don't leave your post, / because calmness alleviates great offenses" (10:4).

Keep silent before the king. Speak to the king regardless. They're both true. It is part of wisdom to discern which is which. How? In dialogue with others. (A good biblical example is when Daniel creates a community of prayer with his three friends to determine God's will [Daniel 2:17-18].)

Passages like these also show us that the Teacher has dropped the pose of being the king and now demonstrates how he has learned to live in the court among rulers. Speaking of which, one bit of advice seems particularly timely in this age of e-mail, texting, Twitters, and Tweets: "Don't curse a king even in private; don't curse the rich in your bedroom, because a bird could carry your voice; some winged creature could report what you said!" (Ecclesiastes 10:20).

I'm reminded of the song by singer Carrie Newcomer "Don't Click Send." In our cyber-age any statement might live forever on YouTube. A chance comment we may not really mean can be passed along to haunt us. Just because we can communicate at the speed of light doesn't mean we ought to. As the Teacher shows, this was true thousands of years ago. It's even truer now.

Just Not Fair

One of the things lamented by the Teacher is that not even wisdom and courage necessarily lead to fame. The Teacher gives a startling example about a poor but wise man who saved a small town from a mighty king who waged war against them. Despite what he had done, "no one remembered that poor man" (Ecclesiastes 9:15). Doing right doesn't always lead to getting credit.

Yet here once again I take the Teacher to task. For isn't this why we honor the unknown soldiers of different conflicts by choosing one as representative of all and raising a shrine to the heroism and sacrifice that can be named only by God?

I find I like both agreeing and arguing with the Teacher, and I invite you to do the same. I couldn't agree more with him when he says, "As dead flies spoil the perfumer's oil, / so a little folly outweighs wisdom and honor" (Ecclesiastes 10:1). But what was true in the Teacher's day—"You don't understand what the life-breath does in the fetus inside a pregnant woman's womb" (11:5)—is no longer true for us, is it? We do know. We've seen. We understand.

He concludes the statement, "so you can't understand the work of God, who makes everything happen" (Ecclesiastes 11:5). Now we can look into the heart of an atom and of a galaxy. If we cannot fully understand the work of God, we can joyfully pull away the layers and at least get a better look at and greater appreciation for all that God has done. The Teacher was wrong. There is something new under the sun. And nothing is newer than the life of the new covenant, brought into being when "the Word became Flesh" (John 1:14).

True, True, True

I laugh when I read, "Through laziness, the roof sags; / through idle hands, the house leaks" (Ecclesiastes 10:18). I am reminded of the lazy man who told the traveling salesman the reason he didn't bother repairing his roof was because when it rained, it was too wet to do so; and when it was dry, his roof was as good as any man's.

Maybe the problem, like the story of the centipede who could no longer walk once someone asked him how he did it, is simply that sometimes we think too much. "See this alone I found: God made human beings straightforward, but they search for many complications" (Ecclesiastes 7:29).

Yet one senses that the Teacher truly draws joy, happiness, or at least good times from contemplation, reflection, and observations about the nature of life. His conclusion seems to be that part of living right is living well, although, as in the third verse below, he sometimes concludes with a downer:

> Feasts are made for laughter,
>> wine cheers the living,
>> and money answers everything. (Ecclesiastes 10:19)

Go, eat your food joyfully and drink your wine happily because God has already accepted what you do. (9:7)

Rejoice, young person, while you are young! Your heart should make you happy in your prime. Follow your heart's inclinations and whatever your eyes see, but know this: God will call you to account for all of these things. (11:9)

About the Scripture

Roll Out the Barrel

Michael M. Homan, Associate Professor of Hebrew Bible at Xavier University of Louisiana in New Orleans and an archaeologist, makes an interesting suggestion about Ecclesiastes 11:1-2. Beer making in ancient Israel involved adding barley bread to water with dates, raisins, and other flavorings, then allowing it to sit for three-to-five days to ferment. Homan thinks that when you "send your bread out on the water," you will find it again as beer! It should then be shared with seven or eight friends, verse 2 suggests, because you never know what disaster may be waiting to strike.

Perhaps the one thing the Teacher accomplishes is to show us the limitations of philosophy. One sees that looking for meaning within the confines of the world without recourse to that One who lies beyond the world and created the world is a dead end. The Teacher is not only closing a door on the limitations of human wisdom, he is perhaps unintentionally opening the door to the new covenant.

And Finally . . .

There is a certainly somber yet poetically beautiful challenge to all of us as the Teacher closes his book in what is both figuratively and literally the final chapter. "Remember your creator in your prime, / before the days of trouble arrive" (Ecclesiastes 12:1), he pleads, before beginning a powerful litany of endings both cosmic and kitchen-based. Sun, moon, stars, and light grow dim; women cease grinding their grain; the birds and the singers fall silent; and terrors haunt the streets because, inevitably, "the human goes to the eternal abode, / with mourners all around in the street" (12:5). And the "dust returns to the earth as it was before / and the life-breath returns to God who gave it" (12:7).

As part of this relinquishing of life, the Teacher uses striking images, saying, "The gold bowl shatters; the jar is broken at the spring" (Ecclesiastes 12:6). Yet even our loss and the disintegration of things does not destroy their beauty or cause us to forget them. The Mogollon, who

About the Christian Faith

Treat—and a Trick!

Is there a modern Christian observance that goes well with Ecclesiastes? Mexican believers and many Americans with Hispanic / Latino roots celebrate an odd church holiday called Dia de los Muertos, or Day of the Dead, as part of All Saints' Day and All Souls' Day. The celebration includes macabre costumes and the eating of candy skulls. Celebrants not only call to mind those who have died, they also remind each other, children included, that we all die. Instead of being a gloomy holiday, it is a frenzied invitation to live life more fully because it is so finite.

lived a thousand years ago in what is now New Mexico, created beautiful black-and-white pottery depicting the creatures who shared their world. When a person died, a hole was punched through the bowl they used; and it was buried with them. When I gaze on what they left behind, its beauty moves me. The figures still tell a story. Their presence in the land of my ancestors still matters.

What beauty will you leave behind? What thought or saying, what thing, will you bequeath to others that will be valued? How will you be remembered? What stories will be told?

The Teacher ends as he began: "Perfectly pointless, says the Teacher, everything is pointless" (Ecclesiastes 12:8). What has followed has been millennia of dialogue and discussion about these wonderfully crafted words.

What do you think this book has revealed about the mind of God? What has it revealed to you about yourself? Why do you think it was preserved and included in the Bible?

Looking Backward

The final seven verses of Ecclesiastes seem to have been written by someone who put the book together in its final form. This writer tells us to take hold of the Teacher's advice to fear God (Ecclesiastes 12:13, compare 5:7b) and sees in it the major teaching of the book. He makes explicit the implicit teaching that while it is true that "everything is the same for everyone" (9:2), God dwells with us, bringing "every deed to judgment, including every hidden thing, whether good or bad" (12:14). We can endure pain, injustice, and frustration because God dwells with us!

This writer also commended the Teacher because he "listened and investigated" (Ecclesiastes 12:9). So many people think they know everything and don't listen to anybody. But when dialogue ceases in the church, when people make pronouncements based on their One-Verse Bibles (Remember those?), then they have left the path of wisdom and have proved the Teacher right in at least one thing: The church will have become perfectly pointless.

Live the Story

Once after a writers' meeting adjourned, I stayed afterward with a fellow writer talking about the big issues of the day. Then I said, "I heard rain is on the way." My companion looked startled; stood up; and abruptly said, "If we're talking about the weather, we're not talking about anything" and left.

I don't know. Maybe he was right. After all, the Teacher does say, "Those who watch the wind blow will never sow, and those who observe the clouds will never reap" (Ecclesiastes 11:4).

I don't remember anything about the important issues we were discussing that day, but I do remember we needed rain. Besides, the Teacher also advises sowing seed and keeping an eye on what happens (Ecclesiastes 11:6). One of his themes is that there's no way to make sense of the big issues, but truth—and therefore God—is found in daily living and daily joy. He keeps coming back to the basics: "Go, eat your food joyfully and drink your wine happily because God has already accepted what you do" (9:7).

How does the perspective of Ecclesiastes help you deal with the pain, injustice, and even the seeming randomness and vexation of life? In what ways does it provide a ground on which you can meet God?

1. From *Hamlet*; Act 1, Scene 3.

8.

The Best Song Ever

Song of Songs 1:1–8:14

Claim Your Story

The poet Christopher Marlowe once asked, "Whoever loved that loved not at first sight?"[1] Thirty-seven years ago as a college junior, I volunteered to be a counselor at Freshman Camp for LaVerne College in California. My future wife was a freshman. I spotted her sitting on a large rock in that mountain camp and immediately knew she was the "one." Later that night I insisted we dance together, despite my clumsiness, and afterward took her out to show her the stars, at least until a skunk walked by and sent us back to our respective cabins! That night I told my college roommate I'd met the woman I was going to marry. Nine months later we said, "I do" despite the fact that we had no money, no jobs, and three years of graduate school ahead. Well, we're still together. That's why, when I read Song of Songs[2], I can say, "They're playing our song!"

Where are you in your journey of love and faith? Do the words of Song of Songs remind you of how you used to feel? Is this how you feel now? Have you ever felt this way about another person? Have you ever felt this way about God?

Enter the Bible Story

If you're driving through Pennsylvania Dutch country, you might come across a souvenir bearing the motto, "Kissing Wears Out. Cooking Don't." Like all folk wisdom, you can probably interpret that saying a couple of ways; but I take it to mean that romantic love is all fine and good, but real love is putting meat and potatoes on the table and money in the bank. Romantic love is dessert. So you'd think that as far as biblical books go, some might consider the Song of Songs, with its celebration of romantic love, to be dessert, as afterthought more than anything else.

But judging from what the ancient rabbis wrote about this book, Song of Songs is the meat and potatoes. Unlike some books of the Bible whose inclusion in the Scriptures was a subject of debate, this little book had no problem making the cut. Not only that, but—well, listen to Rabbi Akiba, who died around the year A.D. 135, who was famed for his wisdom and knowledge: "The whole world is not worth the day on which the Song of Songs was given to Israel for all the writings are holy but the Song of Songs is the holiest of the holy."[3]

All-Time Best

Tell the truth; would you have chosen this book as "the holiest of the holy"? But the title itself hints at this. "Song of Songs" can also be translated "The Greatest Song."

So what are we to think about this, the greatest song?

First, it is passionate. The Common English Bible translators did a wonderful job getting across the frantic, over-the-top quality of lovers who no longer have either foot planted on the ground and whose heads are so stuck in the clouds that you can see their feet waving above you.

The joy of love is present in these lines; but so are the anxiety, the absurdity, the obsession, the wondering, the wandering, the uncertainty, and the certainty that goes along with falling head over heels in love.

The love songs didn't spring out of a vacuum. They are part of a venerable tradition as old as love itself. Parallels of these poems are found in all the ancient cultures.

A Different Viewpoint

If you have read the book, you may have noticed that there is no mention of God. The only other book of the Bible that does not mention God is Esther, though at least Esther uses the language of religious life—fasting, praying, feast days, for instance. Song of Songs does not contain any references to anything approaching a life of worship.

One of the biggest differences between this book and most other books of the Bible is that Song of Songs seems to have been written at least in part by a woman. (Some think the Letter to the Hebrews was written by Priscilla, who along with her husband worked with Paul in Corinth [see Acts 18]. A book some years back by Harold Bloom, *The Book of J*, suggested at least part of Genesis was also written by a woman; but we have no way of knowing for sure.) The Hebrew language, like many others, makes it clear if the speaker is male or female and whether there is one speaker or many. The Common English Bible reflects the changes in the gender and number of speakers in its translation.

Both Proverbs and Ecclesiastes, written by men, have betrayed an unbalanced attitude about what they perceive as the wily snares of women. There is a much higher view of women in Song of Songs. The only other biblical book that comes to mind as showing this much appreciation for women is the Gospel of Luke.

The King James Version translates Song of Songs 1:5 as "I am black, but comely," as if it were unusual for someone to be beautiful if black, perpetuating derogatory stereotypes that would not have been considered true in biblical times. The King James translators lived in a society in which even black hair was considered a flaw and whose previous ruler, Queen Elizabeth, painted her face white to remove any trace of color. However, the Hebrew letter *vav*, when placed before another word, can be translated many ways according to context: "and," "but," "though," "yet," "if," and so forth. The Common English Bible, recognizing the non-European nature of the ancient Middle East and realizing that people who work outdoors get even darker, translates the phrase as "Dark am I, and lovely."

This dark-skinned woman whose poems comprise much of the book and who is the love interest of the male who sings with her teaches us that love is powerful. Thoughts of love consume both waking and sleeping hours. And that includes her dreams.

All I Have to Do Is Dream

That aspect of dream-life fantasy (see especially Song of Songs 3:1-4) is one of the most interesting aspects of these songs. In our era, the whole idea of courtship, of increasing intimacy in stages, catching each other's eye, speaking about, speaking to, holding hands, standing arm in arm, experiencing the first kiss, and so on, is lost in a headlong rush to fulfillment. But in the biblical world, contact between men and women was more strictly regulated. Men and women might only catch glimpses of each other or know each other only through the description given by a relative. The result was that the type of romantic encounters we take for granted today could take place only in dreams or fantasies. The themes of fantasy and dream are a reminder that physical fulfillment of love is only part of love's joys.

In some of the poems, the lover beckons. In others, she or he vanishes, but with the suggestion that the lover will return. In some, the lover is searching for the beloved. Always, there is the praise of love itself.

The poems are sensuous, but they are not graphic. Song of Songs is not a how-to manual. The "pomegranate" (Song of Songs 4:3), the "garden" (4:12), and the "vine" (6:11) are euphemisms meant to suggest the female form without being explicit.

The poems themselves are set in surroundings familiar to anyone: in cultivated countryside as well as in wild habitat, in home interiors as well as in the city streets. In some of the poems, the friends and relatives of the lovers are supportive. But the city streets are the least sympathetic locale in general, and the guards seem menacing.

Comparing your lover's hair to a flock of goats, teeth to a flock of ewes, face to a pomegranate, may strike us as odd; but this is part of a venerable tradition known as the *wasf*. *Wasf* includes poetic descriptions of parts of the body in unlike terms. This doesn't have to make sense; love looks crazy from the outside. Why else would the young man compare his dearest to "a mare among Pharaoh's chariots" (Song of Songs 1:9), and why else would a young woman swoon that her dearest thought of her that way?

Think of love songs that have spoken to your life. Were any of them silly? Under what circumstances did you first hear them? Why are they special? Are the lyrics as bright today as when you first heard them?

Found in Translation

Translation can be difficult. Song of Songs includes Hebrew words that appear nowhere else, and whose meaning is therefore difficult to determine. Some words have more than one meaning. While the Greeks had four different words for love to express different qualities, both English and Hebrew have only one word to cover all the many aspects of love. This allows both richness and ambiguity when talking about love.

Some terms are simply untranslatable. When poet and scholar Marcia Falk published her translation of the Song of Songs, she left 6:12 in Hebrew. That's because, as many have noted, it is not decipherable. Translators simply hit a brick wall on this one and do their best to make sense of it. No doubt, it made perfect sense thousands of years ago. However, language changes; and sometimes it is regional. Until I moved to middle Pennsylvania, I'd never heard the word *yuhns* (you all), nor did I know that the phrase "The pickles is all" means "We're out of pickles."

Don't Pass Over This Song

The Song of Songs is considered part of the third section of the Hebrew Scriptures, known as the Writings. Some of the ancient rabbis, considering the three books they believed to have been authored by Solomon, famed for his wisdom, thought the proper order to be Song of Songs, Proverbs, and Ecclesiastes, representing one's feelings in youth, middle age, and the end of life. But one rabbi insisted that Song of Songs should come last in the sequence because it is the pinnacle.

Song of Songs is also a part of what are known as the Five Festal Scrolls, five short books of the Bible (including Esther, Lamentations, Ruth, and Ecclesiastes) that are read at certain Jewish festivals. As such, each became associated with a particular holiday or observance.

A friend of mine reads *How the Grinch Stole Christmas* every Christmas Eve. It has become a tradition. The children grew up, went off to college, and eventually took jobs; yet they always returned home because for them it just wasn't Christmas without that recitation. In the same way, the Song of Songs is read each year on the sabbath within Passover. And for many people it's not Passover without the Song of Songs.

Is there a book, movie, or song you associate with a holy day? With a significant day in your life involving love? Involving God?

Why the association between these love songs and an action story about horrifying plagues, the angel of death, and the parting of the sea? Some have suggested it's because love was at the heart of God's action in freeing the Hebrew people from slavery in Egypt. And some modern rabbis have suggested that Song of Songs provides an alternative to the violence of Passover; unlike the narrative in Exodus, no one has to die.

These eight brief chapters have inspired mountains of commentary. God's love for us and our love for God over the years became for some the primary, or even only, means of interpreting the book. The second-century theologian Origen wrote extensively about Song of Songs, portraying it as a great drama that told the love story between God and the people. He warned against letting younger people read it because they might overlook its sacred side and focus on physical passion.

The medieval mystic Bernard of Clairvaux took a different tack. Though he wrote many sermons based on Song of Songs in which he sought the sacred side of the text, he insisted the reason we understand God's love in the first place is because this "is the book of our experience."[4]

What are we to think, then, about a book of the Bible that consists of nothing but love songs? Perhaps this is an indication of how important love is to the structure of the universe. First John 4:16 says simply, "God is love." Verse 19 adds, "We love because God first loved us." Jesus himself, when asked to name the greatest law, chose love as the greatest virtue when he said we are to love God with all our heart, being, and mind and to love our neighbor as ourselves (Matthew 22:37-40).

We know God through love. We find God in love. The great mystics have always known this. How many of us consider the love we share with God as being all of a piece with the passion we feel for another, with desire and longing changing the way we look at everything? In both the Old and New Testaments, love and sex are not evil; they are good.

Think of all the energy we put into life as lovers: "chance" meetings, tossing and turning all night, the way a lover can dominate every thought. What did you experience during the height of romantic love? Have you

---

About the Christian Faith

The Song of Songs in the Hymnbook

When it comes to worship, the language of love is nowhere more apparent than in our hymns. Many hymn writers have embraced the language of Song of Songs to describe the love between Jesus and the believer. "Jesus, blessed Jesus, Rose of Sharon / Bloom in radiance / And in love within my heart," wrote Ida A. Guirey in a hymn published in 1922, picking up the image from Song of Songs 2:1. Charles W. Fry referred to Jesus as "The Lily of the Valley" in his hymn "I Have Found a Friend in Jesus" (1881), pulling language from Song of Songs 2:1 and 5:10. Jackson Mason's "O Voice of the Beloved" (1889) draws heavily on the language of Song of Songs 2:10-13.

To read and hear these hymns, go to www.cyberhymnal.org.

---

put that same energy into your life of love with God? Do you try to "run into" God in your daily life? Are there times you are so filled with fascination that you can hardly sleep?

Is there a place for "romantic" love for God and "long-term" or "marriage" love for God? What do you suppose is the quality of God's love for you?

The Payoff

Regardless of its interpretation, Song of Songs does not present a tragic vision of the world; it's filled with joy. Still, these love songs are not frothy pop music; these are gut-wrenching, lay it all on the table, real emotions for real people love songs. Renita Weems, an African American theologian, compares the Song of Song to American blues for its raw, authentic depiction of the highs and lows of love.

A friend of mine who was also my Hebrew teacher in seminary says the Song of Songs is not about "wimpy, sentimental love." It's about "tough love," love tough enough, like Ecclesiastes, to accompany you to the edge of death's mysteries and beyond. Despite the poem's focus on young lovers whose furthest thought is that everything has an end, the

Across the Testaments

A Constant Theme

The intimacy invited by Song of Songs is mirrored in the New Testament understanding of the relationship between Christ and the church. The church, revealed as the New Jerusalem, is described as the bride of Christ (Revelation 21:2). First Corinthians 13 celebrates love's giving and forgiving nature. And when you come right down to it, "love is as strong as death" (Song of Songs 8:6) is just one more way of saying that "nothing can separate us from God's love in Christ Jesus our Lord" (Romans 8:38).

Song of Songs faces death squarely. In the last chapter, the woman asks the man to "set me as a seal over your heart, / as a seal upon your arm" (8:6). People sealed their documents with a personal seal pressed into hot wax. Each seal was as good as a signature. The reason the woman wants to be set as a seal on the heart is that while death is inevitable, death does not mean the end of love.

I read Song of Songs 8:6 at every funeral I perform because of its power and promise, especially in its second line: "for love is as strong as death, / passionate love unrelenting as the grave." The images of fire and water that follow represent the powers of chaos that threaten to dissolve the world we know. Love, however, is more powerful. This is the climax of the book, perhaps even of the whole Bible. It proclaims the triumph of love. The only verse that says it more clearly is 1 Corinthians 13:8: "Love never fails."

Ordinary Life, Extraordinary Love

I was taught in college that in Shakespeare's comedies, love is a disease that can be cured only by marriage. In other words, we need the nitty-gritty of everyday life to knock some sense into us.

Maybe the cynics are right. Maybe the giddiness, the craziness of romantic love, can't be maintained forever. Would we really want to remain foolishly in love forever?

But what if that's the way God feels about us all the time? Are we prepared to meet God with the same ardent feelings—forever?

I've learned at least (and the poets of Song of Songs seem to feel the same way) that relationships founded on love sustain us beyond the spring and summer, into the cold of autumn's aging and winter's death. "Cooking don't wear out." Neither does kissing.

So there.

Live the Story

I asked my evening Bible study group what book they wanted to study next and someone said, "Ecclesiastes." I answered, "Sure, on one condition"—that we study Song of Songs at the same time. And we did. We'd go about twenty minutes on one book, then go to the other, and come back to the first one later.

Why? Because life isn't all "perfectly pointless" as Ecclesiastes says, nor is it all *muchas smoochas* as Song of Songs proclaims. Life is both. It's hard to imagine being in either frame of mind all the time. Taken together, these two very different books give a pretty balanced view of life. Both biblical books speak the truth even though they sometimes sound like total opposites.

How true are they in your life? Are you more of an Ecclesiastes or a Song of Songs person? Are there places in your life where you've sounded more like one than the other?

In your experience, is "love as strong as death"? Why, or why not?

Where is the passion in your life? Where do you pour your heart and soul? How is God honored by your passion?

1. From http://www.poemhunter.com/poem/who-ever-loved-that-loved-not-at-first-sight/. (5-26-11)

2. Although traditionally known as Song of Solomon, modern scholarship has determined that a more appropriate title for this book of the Bible is Song of Songs. The Common English Bible reflects that interpretation in its translation.

3. From http://www.dhushara.com/book/song/song.htm. (5-26-11)

4. From http://www.ts.mu.edu/content/58/58.1/58.1.1.pdf. (5-26-11)

Leader Guide

People often view the Bible as a maze of obscure people, places, and events from centuries ago and struggle to relate it to their daily lives. IMMERSION invites us to experience the Bible as a record of God's loving revelation to humankind. These studies recognize our emotional, spiritual, and intellectual needs and welcome us into the Bible story and into deeper faith.

As leader of an IMMERSION group, you will help participants to encounter the Word of God and the God of the Word that will lead to new creation in Christ. You do not have to be an expert to lead; in fact, you will participate with your group in listening to and applying God's life-transforming Word to your lives. You and your group will explore the building blocks of the Christian faith through key stories, people, ideas, and teachings in every book of the Bible. You will also explore the bridges and points of connection between the Old and New Testaments.

Choosing and Using the Bible

The central goal of IMMERSION is engaging the members of your group with the Bible in a way that informs their minds, forms their hearts, and transforms the way they live out their Christian faith. Participants will need this study book and a Bible. IMMERSION is an excellent accompaniment to the Common English Bible (CEB). It shares with the CEB four common aims: clarity of language, faith in the Bible's power to transform lives, the emotional expectation that people will find the love of God, and the rational expectation that people will find the knowledge of God.

Other recommended study Bibles include *The New Interpreter's Study Bible* (NRSV), *The New Oxford Annotated Study Bible* (NRSV), *The HarperCollins Study Bible* (NRSV), the *NIV and TNIV Study Bibles*, and the *Archaeological Study Bible* (NIV). Encourage participants to use more than one translation. *The Message: The Bible in Contemporary Language* is a modern paraphrase of the Bible, based on the original languages. Eugene H. Peterson has created a masterful presentation of the Scripture text, which is best used alongside rather than in place of the CEB or another primary English translation.

One of the most reliable interpreters of the Bible's meaning is the Bible itself. Invite participants first of all to allow Scripture to have its say. Pay attention to context. Ask questions of the text. Read every passage with curiosity, always seeking to answer the basic Who? What? Where? When? and Why? questions.

Bible study groups should also have handy essential reference resources in case someone wants more information or needs clarification on specific words, terms, concepts, places, or people mentioned in the Bible. A Bible dictionary, Bible atlas, concordance, and one-volume Bible commentary together make for a good, basic reference library.

The Leader's Role

An effective leader prepares ahead. This leader guide provides easy-to-follow, step-by-step suggestions for leading a group. The key task of the leader is to guide discussion and activities that will engage heart and head and will invite faith development. Discussion questions are included, and you may want to add questions posed by you or your group. Here are suggestions for helping your group engage Scripture:

State questions clearly and simply.

Ask questions that move Bible truths from "outside" (dealing with concepts, ideas, or information about a passage) to "inside" (relating to the experiences, hopes, and dreams of the participants).

Work for variety in your questions, including compare and contrast, information recall, motivation, connections, speculation, and evaluation.

Avoid questions that call for yes-or-no responses or answers that are obvious.

Don't be afraid of silence during a discussion. It often yields especially thoughtful comments.

Test questions before using them by attempting to answer them yourself.

When leading a discussion, pay attention to the mood of your group by "listening" with your eyes as well as your ears.

Guidelines for the Group

IMMERSION is designed to promote full engagement with the Bible for the purpose of growing faith and building up Christian community. While much can be gained from individual reading, a group Bible study offers an ideal setting in which to achieve these aims. Encourage participants to bring their Bibles and read from Scripture during the session. Invite participants to consider the following guidelines as they participate in the group:

Respect differences of interpretation and understanding.

Support one another with Christian kindness, compassion, and courtesy.

Listen to others with the goal of understanding rather than agreeing or disagreeing.

Celebrate the opportunity to grow in faith through Bible study.

Approach the Bible as a dialogue partner, open to the possibility of being challenged or changed by God's Word.

Recognize that each person brings unique and valuable life experiences to the group and is an important part of the community.

Reflect theologically—that is, be attentive to three basic questions: What does this say about God? What does this say about me/us? What does this say about the relationship between God and me/us?

Commit to a lived faith response in light of insights you gain from the Bible. In other words, what changes in attitudes (how you believe) or actions (how you behave) are called for by God's Word?

Group Sessions

The group sessions, like the chapters themselves, are built around three sections: "Claim Your Story," "Enter the Bible Story," and "Live the Story." Sessions are designed to move participants from an awareness of their own life story, issues, needs, and experiences into an encounter and dialogue with the story of Scripture and to make decisions integrating their personal stories and the Bible's story.

The session plans in the following pages will provide questions and activities to help your group focus on the particular content of each chapter. In addition to questions and activities, the plans will include chapter title, Scripture, and faith focus.

Here are things to keep in mind for all the sessions:

Prepare Ahead

Study the Scripture, comparing different translations and perhaps a paraphrase.

Read the chapter, and consider what it says about your life and the Scripture.

Gather materials such as large sheets of paper or a markerboard with markers.

Prepare the learning area. Write the faith focus for all to see.

Welcome Participants

Invite participants to greet one another.

Tell them to find one or two people and talk about the faith focus.

Ask: What words stand out for you? Why?

Guide the Session

Look together at "Claim Your Story." Ask participants to give their reactions to the stories and examples given in each chapter. Use questions from the session plan to elicit comments based on personal experiences and insights.

Ask participants to open their Bibles and "Enter the Bible Story." For each portion of Scripture, use questions from the session plan to help participants gain insight into the text and relate it to issues in their own lives.

Step through the activity or questions posed in "Live the Story." Encourage participants to embrace what they have learned and to apply it in their daily lives.

Invite participants to offer their responses or insights about the boxed material in "Across the Testaments," "About the Scripture," and "About the Christian Faith."

Close the Session
Encourage participants to read the following week's Scripture and chapter before the next session.
Offer a closing prayer.

1. Read the Handbook
Proverbs 1–9

Faith Focus
Having reverence for God is the first step in receiving God's gift of wisdom, which helps us avoid potential troubles and live well.

Before the Session
On a large sheet of paper, print the Spanish proverb from the study. Locate a hymnal with the hymn "Softly and Tenderly Jesus Is Calling." Lyrics are also available online at several sites for download. Some sites even include piano accompaniment.

Reflect on what has been the source of wisdom in your life. Has God's wisdom been revealed to you in interactions with other people? Pray that you can help group members encounter God's wisdom and that you will discern God's presence in the group.

Claim Your Story
Call the attention of the group to the Spanish proverb. If a Spanish speaker is present, ask that person to read the proverb aloud; otherwise, read the translation of it from the study. Then ask volunteers to discuss its meaning. Invite the group to share what wisdom they learned from parents and other family members. The writer observes that, like this proverb, biblical wisdom works most of the time. Discuss times when the wisdom participants garnered from family members helped and times when it didn't. When it didn't, what was the reason?

Enter the Bible Story
Ask for a show of hands of those who have previously read the entire Book of Proverbs. If anyone has, what was their impression? If not, are there particular proverbs participants can recall? Why should we read the Book of Proverbs anyway? Do the two reasons cited in the study make sense to the group? Ask volunteers to name the sources from which George Washington derived his rules for living. What sources would group members name as the sources for common sense in their lives?

Ask for the definition in the study for natural religion. Invite a volunteer to read Proverbs 26:4-5 aloud. What does the group make of this seemingly contradictory advice? As the study suggests, ask each person to think of a saying learned as a child. After allowing a few minutes for persons to reflect, ask them to pair up with another person and share their saying, as well as whether it has stood the test of time and in what circumstances it applies.

Invite someone to summarize what the study says about the origin of Proverbs as an "Instruction Manual for Civil Servants." Then ask a volunteer to read aloud Proverbs 1:1-7. Based on this "book jacket blurb," what do participants expect from this book? What does the study indicate is the key ingredient in this book? The study indicates that strict scientific accuracy is not necessary in order for a proverb about the natural world to function as a way we can find God. Do participants agree?

Invite someone to read aloud Proverbs 1:20-21, the introduction of the character "Wisdom." The study compares the city gates with the coffee shop. Invite the group to name places in your own community that are comparable. How might social networking sites function like the city gates?

Wisdom's realm, we are told, is no abstraction but rather the real world where we are confronted with choices between good and evil. Invite the group to discuss the relationship between free choice and fate. Are our own choices determining factors in our lives?

Ask volunteers to read aloud Proverbs 2:16; 5:3-4, 20; 9:13-18. What picture is being painted of the temptress? Would you say these warnings might be applicable to civil servants today? Who is the figure "Folly" (9:13)?

Since Proverbs was originally addressed to young men who were civil servants, give group members a few minutes to think about what would be comparable advice for today's female civil servants. Against whom might an instruction book warn young women?

Discuss the question posed in the study in the last paragraph of this section about how God's Word is to be used and how those ideas differ from the idea of biblical wisdom.

Live the Story

Invite the group to reflect on times in their own lives they failed to heed wisdom that would have led them to make a wise choice. Invite volunteers to share what happened and if possible to cite a saying or proverb that expresses that unheeded wisdom. Why is it so hard to apply proverbs to ourselves?

Encourage group members, as preparation for the next session, to read the first nine chapters of Proverbs at home and identify proverbs in those chapters that apply to them as well as those that do not seem useful.

Close by reading aloud Proverbs 8. Ask the group to listen for similarities to the chapter as you sing the hymn "Softly and Tenderly Jesus Is Calling," substituting "Wisdom" for the name of Jesus.

2. This or That
Proverbs 10–15

Faith Focus
Wisdom helps us live righteously and exercise our freedom in beneficial ways.

Before the Session
On two large sheets of paper, print these headings: "Proverbs That Apply" and "Proverbs That Don't." Place these sheets on tables (or post on the wall) along with felt-tip markers. Also write the two proverbs printed under "Enter the Bible Story"—Proverbs 10:4 and 12:1—on a large sheet of paper.

Claim Your Story
As participants arrive, point them to the titled blank sheets of paper and encourage them to list any proverbs from Chapters 1–9 they identified in their at-home reading. Which of the ones they classify as not applying might be rewritten using different images that speak more clearly of contemporary life?

Distribute sheets of paper and pens or pencils. Ask participants to turn the sheets of paper horizontally and then sketch out a line that represents the pathway of their lives thus far. They then should mark places where they made significant choices that required course corrections. Discuss the questions in the last paragraph of this section in the study about what wisdom guided their course corrections.

Enter the Bible Story
The study identifies Proverbs 10–15, generally attributed to Solomon, as the core of the book. Ask a volunteer to define antithetical sayings; then refer the group to the two that you posted. Divide the group into two small groups, and assign one of the proverbs to each group. Ask participants to take the study writer's suggestion to interpret their assigned proverb in the light of their own experience. Then ask them to pair up with a person who explored the other proverb and share their ideas. How do they respond to the questions posed by the study?

Assign one or more participants to each of the six chapters of Proverbs in this session. Give participants highlighters, and ask them to read their assigned chapter and highlight proverbs that intrigue them. In the total group, ask them to read aloud the proverbs they highlighted. Which are Brazil nuts? Which are peanuts?

A recurring theme in Proverbs is establishing justice for the purpose of maintaining order. Ask someone to read aloud Proverbs 15:25 and another volunteer to read Luke 18:1-8. Compare these verses with the "real" Golden Rule as stated in the study. What is the difference between approaching a situation with heart as the ancient world defined it and separating rational thought from emotions? Define "the fear of the Lord." When—if ever—have participants had a glimpse of God's true glory? What experiences brought forth that sense of awe? Encourage participants as they continue through this study to underline or highlight verses that include the phrase "the fear of the Lord" and to reflect on similarities and differences in the verses.

Invite participants to select one of the proverbs the study writer chose at random in this section and read the proverb without reading the writer's commentary. After giving them time to reflect on the proverb, have them jot down a couple of sentences of commentary that connect to that proverb and relate to their life experience. Then ask them to read what the study has to say about the proverb. How closely did their own observations jibe with what the study writer said? Ask volunteers to share what they wrote.

One of the central concerns of Proverbs is that lessons learned in the past need to be communicated to the next generation to ensure the stability and safety of a society built on the fear of the Lord. Discuss the questions posed by the study about the trust of succeeding generations. Ask whether the group thinks there are emerging aspects of life in contemporary society for which there may need to be new insights about wisdom. Is it possible that all situations of daily living can be addressed with the wisdom of the past? Allow some time for group members to write their own proverb on self-control, as the study writer suggests. Share participants' proverbs.

Live the Story

Ask the group to consider the questions posed in the study about making contact between generations. How might adults create the kind of environment where wisdom can be shared? What inhibits this kind of environment? Have group members had experiences similar to the writer's, where wisdom shared was initially disdained by an adolescent, only to bear fruit later? Is it possible for the younger generation to have wisdom about some aspect of contemporary life that can be shared with their elders?

Close by inviting participants to share a maxim or proverb their parents offered in the past that came to have meaning for them in later years.

3. If the Shoe Fits...
Proverbs 16:1–22:16; 25:1–29:27

Faith Focus
Wisdom helps us maintain our commitment to righteousness even when the fruits of righteousness are not apparent.

Before the Session
On a large sheet of paper, make a simple timeline that places both Solomon and Hezekiah in context: Solomon (reigned 961–922 B.C.), Divided Kingdom (922–587/86 B.C), Hezekiah (reigned 715–687 B.C.). If you like, add other dates, such as the fall of the Northern Kingdom (Israel) in 722/21 B.C and the fall of the Southern Kingdom (Judah) in 587/86 B.C.

On another large sheet of paper, print "Claiming a Proverb."

On five separate large sheets of paper, print each of the five proverbs identified in the study as the first five seen on the scroll. Plan to place each sheet on a separate table, or display them on the wall at intervals around your space. Provide a red felt-tip marker and a green felt-tip marker with each sheet (or any two colors available).

Claim Your Story
As participants arrive, point them to the sheet headed "Claiming a Proverb" and encourage them to list a proverb from Chapter 25 that speaks to them. Invite them to say why that proverb resonated with them.

Enter the Bible Story
Point out for the group the timeline you posted that gives the dates when the two great kings, Solomon and Hezekiah, reigned. Note that Israel split into the Northern Kingdom (Israel) and the Southern Kingdom (Judah) after Solomon's death and that Hezekiah, who reigned over the Southern Kingdom, saw the fall of the Northern Kingdom.

The portions of Proverbs in this chapter of the study focus on maintaining the social order.

Ask for volunteers to read aloud Proverbs 25:21-22, Romans 12:19-21, and Matthew 5:44. The study refers to the event commemorating the experiences of the prisoners of war at Andersonville, but we have our own recent history of implicit policies that led to the use of torture. Do participants agree or disagree that long-term peace and stability can result from unexpectedly kind behavior? Can the social order be upheld by gently turning the world upside down? When would they say that the nonviolent approach is viable—or is war always the answer? Ask the group what their experience has been when there is conflict within your community of faith. Has there ever been a time in a church conflict when someone has experienced the healing power of words, or are words more often used to wound?

Ask someone to explain briefly John W. Miller's idea that ancient people would have studied Proverbs in groups of five proverbs from the rolled-up scroll. The first five proverbs people would have seen when the scroll was unrolled are found in Proverbs 16:2-6. Point out the five sheets of paper around your space, one for each of these proverbs. Invite group members each to select one sheet and start the following process: They are to read the proverb on that sheet and the commentary in the study. Then each person is to use a green marker to record on the sheet they have selected any comments they have and use a red marker to print unanswered questions. Each person should move from sheet to sheet, reading comments and questions and adding their own. When everyone has had a chance to reflect on all five proverbs, discuss comments or questions that have arisen. As the study suggests, then encourage participants to choose five other proverbs on which to reflect.

Note for the group that the sections of Proverbs we are studying in this session reveal some consistent themes having to do with economic realities. The Hezekiah section (25:1–29:27) notes what a reforming king should do. Distribute paper and pencils or pens. Challenge the group to come up with a job description for an ideal king based on this passage. After a few minutes, ask volunteers to read their descriptions.

Focus on the section dealing with folly. The study writer notes that sometimes the sky is falling and sometimes it's just Chicken Little. In what ways in our recent history beginning with 9/11 have we experienced this? How has our 24/7 news cycle, as well as social networking, e-mail, and sites like Twitter, increased the potential for folly through rumor and gossip? Is it possible to take the long view, as Proverbs invites us to do, in this environment? *mayberry ~ Gossip*

Live the Story

Invite the group to spend a few minutes using Proverbs as a mirror, as the study suggests. Ask participants to reflect in silence on the questions in the last paragraph.

4. True, Reliable Words
Proverbs 22:17–24:34

Faith Focus
Holy living involves not only faith in God but also learning from the experience of believers who have gone before us.

Before the Session
Go to www.teachingvalues.com/goldenrule.html to find "The Universality of the Golden Rule in the World Religions." Print the versions from several world religions on a large sheet of paper. Reflect on people in your life who have demonstrated wisdom in settling disputes or in dealing with challenges related to the issues addressed by Proverbs in this session. What principles guided their approach to thorny issues?

Claim Your Story
Divide your group into teams of two or three. Then invite participants to share stories they can recall from their families or from your church about people who, like the study's example of Farmer Mel, demonstrate a wiser way to settle disputes. Together, discuss what common approaches seem to emerge from the stories. If time allows, have someone read aloud 1 Kings 3:16-28. How did Solomon demonstrate wisdom in settling this dispute?

Enter the Bible Story
Call the attention of the group to the versions of the Golden Rule from world religions. This saying is a common thread of wisdom across many cultures, religions, and times. Invite volunteers to read the versions aloud. Does the universality of the saying diminish its power in any way?

Note for the group that the proverbs in this section have their roots in ancient Egypt and that wisdom, unlike other forms of revelation, intertwines itself among cultures. In contrast to the Egyptian version of these sayings, the Hebrew versions affirm that God takes the part of the poor. In Hebrew society, the redeemer was the family member who stood up for those who were wronged.

Discuss the questions in the study about resources for serving the poor. How do participants engage in this service? Do they focus on agencies or activities that provide direct service only or on activities that address the underlying inequities that contribute to poverty? How does the group respond to the startling image that God will press the life out of those who oppress the poor? Do we make it our business to know about judicial practices that may suppress, ignore, or deny evidence of innocence? Discuss the questions in the study about the court system and how it works.

Invite a volunteer to read aloud Proverbs 23:1-9 and Proverbs 22:26-27. Ask the group to reflect on whether or not they live beyond their means. What impact, if any, does this have on those who are poor? Why are so many people in our society obsessed with owning more and more stuff? What are the implications? How is the rest of the world impacted by the fact that we consume an inordinate amount of the world's resources?

Ask participants to quickly scan the material in the study on the topics of discipline, addictive behavior, sexual misconduct, honoring parents, delight in the misfortune of others, and laziness. Encourage them to choose one of these topics to focus on for a few minutes. Ask them to read the Scripture passage and the accompanying material carefully and spend some time reflecting on the questions posed by the study writer. After a few minutes, suggest that each person find someone who reflected on a topic different from theirs and discuss their thoughts briefly.

Together, talk about how dealing with these issues with wisdom contributes to a more stable society. Then consider the questions at the end of this section posed by the study writer. What lessons seem the most useful? What issues not addressed by Proverbs are crucial to a stable, just society?

Live the Story

Invite the group to return to the persons who were central to the stories they shared at the beginning of the session—those who demonstrated the "wisdom of Solomon" in settling a dispute in family, church, or community or someone who showed great wisdom in struggling with addiction issues or dealing with a debt or in disciplining a young person. If a proverb comes to mind from this session or earlier sessions that this person's actions seem to exemplify, invite them to consider that. Pray the following prayer, inviting participants to name aloud or in their hearts the issue and the person whose actions were wise:

Holy God, we give thanks for the wisdom revealed in many cultures, times, and places. Especially we give thanks for the wisdom of Proverbs. Today we offer special thanks for those persons whose actions revealed your wisdom in difficult situations: For _____, who demonstrated wisdom by _____ (allow a time of silence in which persons and issues can be named aloud). Amen.

5. Words Tried and True
Proverbs 30:1–31:31

Faith Focus
Faith is not a matter of certainty, but of accepting the mystery of God and doing the work at hand.

Before the Session
Do an Internet search on organizations that make microloans, such as the Grameen Foundation (www.grameenfoundation.org). Also visit www.un.org/millenniumgoals/ and read about how the status of women affects families. Locate the old hymn "Sing Them Over Again to Me," which is available online on several lyric sites. Print the words of the first verse and the refrain on a large sheet of paper and post them. Head another large sheet of paper "The Little Moments of Life." Obtain colored self-stick notes and pens or pencils.

Claim Your Story
Ask participants to think about the seemingly insignificant times in their day-to-day lives for which they often wish they had advice. Have them jot these down on the self-stick notes and attach them to the sheet. Read them aloud. How many deal with household or family issues? How many are work related? Which ones deal with leisure time? Together, regroup the notes on the sheet according to these categories and label them.

Enter the Bible Story
The study writer speculates that Agur, whose proverbs make up Chapter 30, may have also been the compiler of Chapter 31. Ask someone to summarize what the study has to say about Agur.

Do participants agree with Agur that faith is not faith if we really know everything? The study writer observes that the ancients dealt with the mysteries of life by staying the course in the small, day-to-day tasks. Invite the group to consider the questions they jotted on the self-stick notes. How important is it to live fully in the present, seeking to perform those small tasks with wisdom?

Ask participants to name television evangelists or religious pundits who seem to know all the answers. How do participants respond to this kind of certainty? Is complete certainty about biblical interpretation possible? Is it advisable?

Recruit several readers to read aloud the counting proverbs in Chapter 30: verses 7-9, 15-16, 18-19, 21-23, 24-28, 29-31 as the group listens. When the verses have been read, have the readers reread the beginning phrases (that is, "Two things I ask of you," "Three things are too wonderful for me," and so forth). Challenge the group to come up with other examples from their own lives that communicate the same sense as each of the counting proverbs.

The study writer observes that our society sometimes confuses lack of responsibility and accountability with freedom. In contrast, Agur has a deep respect for God's commandments and asserts that these laws provide boundaries that allow the freedom for authentic and secure life. Agur suggests that people need to remain in their station in life in order to ensure stability and peace. How does the group react to that? Discuss, as the study suggests, some of the radical shifts in society that have occurred in our lifetimes. How has the shift in the status of women or of people of color affected the society? Can a society have real stability when some of its members are pushed to the margins? Read aloud Proverbs 31:1-9. What is the true responsibility of the rich and powerful in both assuring the rights of the vulnerable and maintaining peace and stability?

Ask participants to read Proverbs 31:10-31. Does this section create a stereotype of women hemmed in by the household, as some have charged, or portray a competent wife in control of the finances and household business, as the study writer suggests? Invite someone to read the passages from Luke cited in the study section "Keeping It All in Order." Share the information about microloans and the impact of the status of women on raising the general well-being of families. How do the facts about women in biblical times revealed in the Luke passages and the information about the status of women illuminate these verses in Proverbs?

Live the Story

Call to the group's attention the paragraph that observes that while nuggets of wisdom in Proverbs do not solve any of life's great mysteries, they do give us tools to live authentically. Invite participants to page through the Book of Proverbs and choose one proverb that has been or is particularly meaningful to them. Then sing the first verse of the old hymn "Sing Them Over Again to Me," pausing after the verse to allow each participant to read his or her chosen proverb. Then sing the hymn's refrain. Give thanks for the "wonderful words of life" in Proverbs, words that represent the collective wisdom of people over many centuries and reveal God's guidance for us today.

6. Been There. Done That. Bought the T-Shirt.

Ecclesiastes 1:1–6:12

Faith Focus

With courage and faith in God, we can forge meaning and purpose out of life, even when life is confusing.

Before the Session

Do some Internet research on the Jewish festival of Sukkot. One reliable site is Judaism 101 (www.jewfaq.org/holiday5.htm). On a large sheet of paper or on a chalkboard or markerboard placed where everyone can see it, print the following open-ended questions: "When I first realized everything dies, including me, I ..."; "When I'm feeling sad or down, I ..." If you like, also download the Kansas song "Dust in the Wind" from iTunes; or get a copy of the lyrics.

As you prepare for this session, consider for yourself the questions in the study under "Claim Your Story." Is a struggle with sadness a significant part of your faith life? How do you cope with the tough questions of living?

Claim Your Story

Invite participants to respond to the open-ended questions you posted. Discuss their responses. How did they feel? What did they do? Does the group consider sadness part of the Christian journey, or do participants feel that somehow Christians should not be sad?

Ask someone to read aloud the first two paragraphs of the study where the writer relates what the child at nursery school said. Invite participants to say how they might have responded to her. Would they have felt uncomfortable and ignored her outburst? Would they have attempted to redirect her attention? Would they have responded some other way? Why is it hard to talk about the inevitability of death?

Enter the Bible Story

Summarize the information in the study about the Jewish festival of Sukkot. Add any additional information you obtained. In this session and in the next session, the group will explore the Book of Ecclesiastes, which the study tells us is unlike anything else in Scripture. Together participants will find out why such a book would be read as part of a festival of joy.

On a large sheet of paper or on a chalkboard or markerboard, list the classic questions of journalism: "Who? What? When? Where? Why?" Invite the group to scan the materials in the study to find who wrote the book, what it's about (Plot? Storyline? Other?), when it was written, and why. Discuss how the study says Wisdom Literature in the Bible works. Why is it important for readers to be in dialogue with this book rather than just being passive listeners or readers?

If possible, play the song "Dust in the Wind"; or simply read the lyrics. Do participants agree with the Teacher that everything passes away, or would they side with the study writer? Why? What would they say endures? Discuss the Teacher's contention that individuals—the lives they have led, their accomplishments and failures—are forgotten. Invite the group to think about friends and family members they have known and loved who are now gone. What are the ways they keep alive the memories of these people? Why is companionship and mutual care—the solace and comfort of relationships—essential for meaning-making in life?

Divide the group into two smaller groups and read Ecclesiastes 3:1-8 aloud as a responsive litany. Have the first group read the first phrase in each verse, while the second reads the concluding phrase. Now ask each group in turn to read aloud just their own portion of the opposite pairs of experiences. What is the impact of hearing these opposites in isolation? Would the group agree with the Teacher that nothing changes? If not, what changes have they observed?

The study writer recounts several stories about the impact of Ecclesiastes either on the lives and perceptions of people or as an influence on artistic expression. Encourage participants to share experiences in their lives where they have seen the lasting impact of joy and affirmation of life in the face of pain and hardship.

Live the Story

Ask someone to read aloud Ecclesiastes 1:5; then have someone else read Psalm 19:5. These two passages reveal a startling contrast in terms of how the same natural phenomenon is perceived. Does a person's outlook shape how he or she experiences even very difficult situations? Ask the group to call to mind a sad or difficult experience such as the study writer recounts in his description of the death of a beloved pet. What difference does it make, for example, if one is able to honor the life of a family member, friend, or even a pet by recalling the blessings of that life?

Encourage the group to pray that trust and faith in God will enable them not only to endure the difficult experiences, but to see them as a part of life.

7. Nothing's Forever, and Everything's Eternal
Ecclesiastes 7:1–12:14

Faith Focus
Being honest about the pain, injustice, and even the seeming randomness and vexation of life provides a ground on which we can meet God.

Before the Session
On a large sheet of paper, print the saying from the study in English and Spanish and post it. On sheets of posterboard or large sheets of paper, make simple outlines of a gravestone for each participant. Obtain pencils and felt-tip markers.

Are the participants in this group mostly older persons who have perhaps done some serious thinking about the inevitability of death? Has anyone recently experienced the loss of a partner or other family member? Is there a young adult who may have lost a child to stillbirth or miscarriage? These life experiences will shape the discussion the group will have.

Claim Your Story
Call the group's attention to the saying you posted. Invite them to volunteer bits of folk wisdom received from others or shared by them during tough times. Do these sayings seem to offer important truths, or are they just clichés that people resort to when they don't know what else to say? Discuss with the group whether the fact that nothing lasts forever can diminish one's joy in living or life's brevity makes it all the more sweet. What do participants think?

Enter the Bible Story
While the study writer agrees with some of the Teacher's wisdom, he takes issue with other aspects. Invite the group to consider the following passages: Ecclesiastes 7:1-12; 10:1-4, 8-20; 11:1-4, where there are parallel statements of Hebrew poetry in which the second statement echoes the first. Ask them to read these verses and to identify a statement with which they agree; one with which they would take issue; and one that is puzzling, obscure, or mystifying. Then pair up or form small groups of three or four to discuss the choices. In the total group, discuss: Were there verses with which some participants agreed and some with which participants took issue? How did the group respond to the "wisdom" expressed about women? Did the group find other places where the Teacher contradicted himself? What is the danger of the One-Verse Bible approach when considering Ecclesiastes—or for that matter, any book of the Bible? What is the value of exploring Scripture in a group?

The study writer observes that there is something new under the sun: the life of the new covenant, birthed when the Word became flesh. He states that looking for meaning within the confines of the world without taking into account the One who created the world is a dead end. Is this true for the members of the group? How does the reality of the new covenant in Jesus Christ transform or break open the limitations of human wisdom?

Invite the group to close their eyes and listen as you read aloud (or have a volunteer read) Ecclesiastes 12:1-7. Tell the group that you will pause after each image to allow them to visualize it clearly. When the reading is finished, invite the group to share which images were the most vivid and communicated most powerfully about life's endings. Discuss, as the study suggests, what things, stories, or sayings group members think they will leave behind to those who come after them.

Ask the group to read silently the last verses of the book, Ecclesiastes 12:8-14. The study writer observes that these verses were added by an editor, someone who compiled the book. This writer states clearly that God's presence—the Word made flesh and dwelling among us—makes pain, injustice, and frustration bearable. How does the group respond?

Live the Story

Call the attention of the group to the sidebar "Treat—and a Trick!" in the study. Tell them that the Day of the Dead focuses on gatherings of family and friends to pray for and remember friends and family members who have died. Families often visit the graves of the deceased and decorate them with gifts and favorite foods. Remind the group of the contrasting image in Chapter 6 in the study of bare tombstones, their writing worn away by wind and weather, lying neglected in a weed-filled graveyard. Distribute the posterboard sheets or large sheets of paper and pencils and felt-tip markers. Invite the group to work singly or in pairs to add to their gravestones, in the spirit of the Day of the Dead, some of the sayings, stories, or other memories they would like to bequeath to coming generations.

Close by inviting the group to reflect on the questions in the final paragraph of this chapter in the study. Pray that Ecclesiastes can provide a ground where participants can meet God.

8. The Best Song Ever
Song of Songs 1:1–8:14

Faith Focus
The gush of feelings associated with spring love cannot survive at that intensity forever; but it can get us started in a relationship that blesses us and warms us all the way through winter's cold, until the day death parts us.

Before the Session
On a large sheet of paper, print the quote from Rabbi Akiba (from the second paragraph of the "Enter the Bible Story" section of the study) and post it. Also print "Wasf" in the center of another large sheet of paper. Obtain several other versions of the Bible, including the NRSV. Get copies of the hymn "The Church's One Foundation." Arrange to have Internet access for the session; or go in advance to the website referred to in this chapter in the study, www.cyber-hymnal.org, and print the lyrics as directed below. Also, have a markerboard and a marker or chalkboard and chalk ready for the group discussion of the meaning of the word *love.*

Claim Your Story
Invite group members to share stories of how they first met a spouse, partner, or significant other. Discuss the questions included in the study. When participants read the Song of Songs, would they say, as does the writer, "They're playing our song!"? Why, or why not?

Enter the Bible Story
Who in the group has previously read the Song of Songs? What were the circumstances? Did anyone read the book as an adolescent because it seemed forbidden—something to make the adults they knew uncomfortable? If so, how did the imagery strike them? Was it erotic, or did it seem confusing or amusing? Call their attention to the quote from Rabbi Akiba. Would the group have identified the Song of Songs as the holiest book? Why, or why not? What do participants make of the absence of mention of God in this book?

This book has a different perspective, perhaps because it seems to have been written, at least in part, by a woman. Invite the group to scan the book and contrast what they read with the view of women revealed in Proverbs and Ecclesiastes. How are women presented in the Song of Songs?

Ask volunteers to read Song of Songs 1:5 from several versions of the Bible (The King James and the Common English Bible translations are included in the study.). How does the study writer account for the use in the King James Version of the conjunction "but," a translation that renders the phrase in the verse derogatory?

In ancient culture, dream-life fantasy was the only way romantic encounters could take place, since interactions between men and women were strictly regulated. In many traditional cultures today, the same is true. Invite the group to contrast this way of controlling courtship with the way romantic love progresses in our society today. What are the advantages to a culture like ours with little or no boundaries on interactions between men and women? What are the disadvantages?

Call the attention of the group to the word *wasf* and invite someone to define the term. Together, scan through the Song of Songs and have participants call out some of the poetic descriptions of body parts. List these on the sheet of paper on which you have written "Wasf." Then ask participants to name love songs, perhaps one named as "our song" in a romantic relationship. Discuss the questions about love songs. Also consider contemporary love songs. Are such lyrics more honest, or are they offensive?

Print "love" on a markerboard or chalkboard and challenge the group to call out sentences that illustrate the many nuances of the meaning of the word. Like English, Hebrew has only one word for love, allowing for both richness and ambiguity. The study writer observes that there are some Hebrew words in the Song of Songs that are found nowhere else and therefore are difficult to translate. What are some regional phrases in your area that might mystify people in another region of the country? Are there phrases or idioms from the past, like "the cat's pajamas," that may have little meaning today?

Note that in the Jewish tradition, the Song of Songs is read every year on the sabbath that falls in Passover. Ask someone to read aloud the paragraph from the study beginning, "Why the association between these love songs and an action story about horrifying plagues?" (in the subsection "Don't Pass Over This Song"). How does the group respond to this explanation?

Distribute the lyrics (or go to the website) of some of the hymns describing the love between Jesus and the believer. Discuss the questions in the study about romantic love for God.

Live the Story
Take a straw poll on this question: Are you an Ecclesiastes kind of person or a Song of Songs person? Invite the group to reflect in silence on the questions in the study about the passion in their lives and whether God is honored by their passion. Close by singing the first verse of "The Church's One Foundation."

Russ Still
moonshiners